WRITE WITHIN YOURSELF

AN AUTHOR'S COMPANION

BY WILLIAM KENOWER

WDBK Editions
Seattle WA 2013

Cover Design by Greg Simanson
Cover Image by Jennifer Paros

PRINTISBN 9780985389406

For further information regarding permissions, please contact wdbk1@comcast.net.

Library of Congress Control Number: 2013933920

For Jen:
Because every book
should begin in love.

CONTENTS

ACKNOWLEDGMENT

I would like to thank the Pacific Northwest Writers Association for their enthusiastic support of a guy who really didn't know what he was doing.

WRITE WITHIN YOURSELF

MANY YEARS AGO I READ AN ARTICLE about the American middle distance runner Alan Webb, whose high school coach described him as having the ability to "run within himself." This is a high compliment for a runner, signifying that while training, the athlete runs neither too fast nor too slow, having become so attuned to his own body that he can confidently and even comfortably push himself to the furthest edge of his stamina.

Reading this, I thought, "That's how I want to write." Lately, I had begun to feel as if I were leaving myself while writing. I suppose I was headed off in search of what I should write about or, worse yet, some proof that what I was writing was "good." This was a very uncomfortable way to write, and the more I thought about it, an equally uncomfortable way to live. Yet there seemed to be no easy trick to keep my attention where it needed to be. My attention could wander as quickly as thought, and soon there I'd be, not writing, only wandering, having already forgotten how I became so lost.

This book is not a guide, but a companion. A guide would tell you where to go. As a writer, only you can ever know that. A good companion, however, can remind you that not only aren't you alone, but that forgetting where you want to go is different than not knowing where you want to go.

I hope these little essays and stories will help remind you that you have always known where you want to go. It's true, you know. But knowing something is not the same as acting on it. If you are like me, you can never be reminded often enough what it feels like to write and live within yourself. If you are like me, the temptation to leave yourself and chase the siren song of praise or run from the hounds of criticism remains. No matter. If my life has taught me anything, it is that there is neither such a thing as too far from myself nor such a thing as too close. The door to our heart remains ever open to our attention, and once within it, we can travel as deeply as we wish, that well-being the only channel through which life is ever known.

WHAT WE WANT MOST

WHEN BOOK PEOPLE, either professional or casual enthusiasts, get together, they often find themselves talking about "great books." Hemingway said he knew he had read a great book if he felt changed after reading it. I think everyone who reads regularly has experienced this. However, whether the great books you talk about are your own personal list, or the canon with which we're all familiar, I would encourage you not to discuss them as if they were somehow a triumph of craft. I have nothing against craft, I edit a magazine full of articles on craft, but a book that stays with us for years after we've read it is much more than mere craft. In almost every case, great books are the result of three things: people who love to write, writing what they most want to write, in the way they most want to write it.

A great book is a work of love—not craft, not intelligence, not discipline, but love. And that love expresses itself in this question asked and answered over and over again: What do I most want to say? A sentence can be grammatically correct, it can be intellectually correct, but if it is not what the author most wanted to say, then it is incorrect. Every day when writers sit down to write, they must ask themselves this question of, "What do I most want to say?" over and over again.

You can try to ask yourself, "What should I write that will sell a lot of books?" or, "What should I write that will win me a lot of awards?" but these questions, tempting and even practical as they seem, are unanswerable. The answers to these questions lie in the hearts of other people, in a writer's potential readers or critics or agents and editors. I can no more know what anyone else desires most in a book, than anyone else can tell me what I most want to write. Whether we like it or not, we are all choosing our own way, and the sovereignty of the soul, of the heart, is absolute. There is no one in the world who can tell us, even if we wanted them to, what we most want. We always have to go find that answer ourselves. And sometimes we find it in the books we write, and in the books we read.

For instance, Deb Caletti told me that when she decided at the age of thirty-two that it was finally time to pursue what was literally a life-long dream of being a writer, she posted a quote by Nietzsche on the wall she faced while writing. The quote read, "Become the person you are." Not, "You will sell a half million copies of your first book." Not, "You are a great writer." It was, "Become the person you are," because she felt that by choosing not to write, as she had for many years, she was avoiding who she truly was. She was avoiding herself. And by going into herself and locating what she most wanted to do—write—she had also located the source for the answer to the question, "What do I most want to write?" And as she answered this question, book-by-book, page-by-page, word-by-word, she was guiding herself toward who she was. She was taking the only route available, by asking the question, what do I most want, what do I most want, what do I most want?

Life, and well-being, is really as simple as that, except for this one small detail: that question remains the most courageous, the most meaningful, and also the most frightening question you will ever answer. If you answer it authentically, there is a good chance you will be pointed in a direction that no one you know has ever traveled before. If you answer it authentically, you may be steered away from family and friends. And as a writer, if you answer it authentically you may see a combination of words on the page that you have never read before, which is both exhilarating and frightening. What if nobody likes it? What if no one will publish it? What if the reviews stink? You don't get to know. Because if you answer this question authentically, you are inevitably guided toward the unknown.

When I had arrived at a point in my life where I knew it was time to reach out to the local writing community, I went to the poet and novelist David Wagoner who teaches at Richard Hugo House in Seattle and showed him something of mine. He read it, and then asked me what I wanted to do, and I told him I wanted to write books, and he said, "I wish you well. It's a lonely road."

And it is sometimes, but it would be far lonelier if I were the only one on it. There is a reason the Hero's Journey is an enduring story archetype. And there is a reason we share these stories of a hero going on a journey of discovery into the unknown. We don't share these stories to learn the way. No story, no teacher, no friend, can show us the way, because they cannot answer the question of what we want most. I believe everyone wants nothing more than to answer this question authentically, but we are all frightened at one point or another to do so; or we believe that pursuing what we love most is somehow meaningless or trivial or even selfish. But I also believe that a really good story reminds us that this journey is meaningful and worth it, and often that's all we need to once again answer the question, "What do I want most?"

WAITING

FOR MANY YEARS I WAITED. It was my profession, but not my chosen profession. I was waiting because I had to wait. My chosen profession was writing, but I was waiting to sell something, for the world of publishers and agents to give me what I wanted, and so in the meantime, while I waited, I waited, and I was often unhappy.

While waiting, I served people. The easiest to serve were the people who knew the world brought them what they wanted. They forgave mistakes and assumed success, for they knew that whatever they asked for would come in time. The worst were those who did not trust the world to bring them what they wanted. They were looking for errors to prove the crowded world where the best tables were taken, the crowded world where orders were lost, would forget about them once again, and they would have to wait and wait to get what they wanted.

It was my job to serve them all, to bring the trusting and the untrusting alike what they wanted. I hated the fear that lay behind the untrusting's eyes. Did they not understand what a miserable life they were creating for themselves by not trusting that what they wanted would come? We called them Customers From Hell.

I needed to reassure the CFH that what they wanted would come. At first, I did this with ruthless efficiency. I still feared the CFH, but what they wanted came so fast and so accurately that they would not have time or reason to complain and spread their hellish view of the world. But efficiency driven by fear eventually undoes itself, and a plate is dropped, a steak overcooked. The CFH would blame me for not caring about them, and I would blame them for spreading their hellishness, and everyone was unhappy.

Then one day I decided to stop waiting. What I wanted was larger than anything a publisher or agent could bring me: I wanted anything I watered to grow. I saw then that I had watered the job of waiter, and it had grown. If I could grow something I didn't love, then I could just as easily grow something I did, but I could not wait for anyone to tell me whether or not the water was being wasted.

There was a short time after I had stopped waiting where I was still a server. These were the best and easiest months of all the years I had spent as a server, and I was often happy. I made more money than I had ever made and experienced diners began telling me I was the finest server they had ever had. When I approached a new table, instead of efficiency I would bring reassurance that everything these strangers wanted would come to them.

And sometimes these strangers would look up at me for the first time and something new would dawn on their faces: recognition. It was just that, as if I were a friend come to visit. We all want to see our friends, for they are the ones we love the most, and with our attention, with time spent together, that friendship grows. Hell is an unfriendly place where nothing grows. The light by which I found my way out of hell was bright enough for others to see, bright enough to recognize as the same light everyone is asking for. If the strangers were happy to see me, it was not because I had arrived to serve them, but to serve the light.

FOUR REASONS

I DON'T THINK WRITING is intrinsically hard. I understand that people find it hard all the time, as have I, but there are always reasons for this, and by my count, usually one of four:

1. You don't actually want to write. Maybe the idea of being a writer appeals to you intellectually, but the writing itself brings you little actual pleasure. There is no crime in this. There are lots of things in the world to do, and writing is by no means the noblest. Find what you truly love most and do it all you can.

2. You are writing the wrong thing. You think you should write something commercial, but you want to write something literary; or you think you should write something literary, but you would rather write a thriller. Or you are trying to write what you think will please an agent or an editor or your writing group or your mother. You are the only one you need to please, and anything can sell, and people don't actually know what they like until they see it. In short, everything is on the table, so pick what makes you happiest, what comes the easiest.

3. You are impatient. No matter how disciplined you are, there is no forcing the river. Whether you write two drafts or ten, you have no choice but to allow the work to come at the rate it wants to come. Patience is required not just to see long projects like novels all the way through, but sentence by sentence. Sometimes waiting another thirty seconds for the full idea to bloom can make all the difference. And oddly, I have found that the more patient I am, the more I am willing to wait, the quicker the work comes.

4. **You are holding two contradictory ideas**. For instance, I want to make a nice living, *but* nobody reads my kinds of books. I love to write, *but* the publishing industry is capricious and uncaring. I love to write, *but* I'm just not talented enough to be published. One idea is going one way, the other idea is going in the exact opposite direction. You in the meantime remain stuck between these competing ideas, convinced they can both be true. Choose what you want to believe and believe only in it, evidence be damned. Evidence, in my experience, changes precisely to align with whatever I believe the most.

THE COWORKER

MANY ARTISTS, particularly beginning artists, complain about their propensity to procrastinate. If only I weren't such a procrastinator, they moan, I would get so much more work accomplished. You can't argue with that, but the procrastinator seems to feel that this procrastination is a kind of disease he or she caught some time back and has been unable to shake ever since.

Of course, procrastination is not a disease at all, but a choice, only in my opinion a very wise choice—the wisest possible, usually, given the circumstances. And what are those circumstances? Waiting for the procrastinator in her workspace is a kind of irritating coworker. Sometimes he is quiet, but usually and eventually he will begin to talk while you work, often posing rhetorical questions, such as, "Why do you think you'll ever finish this book?" or, "Why do you think that's any good?"

Who could work under such conditions? If you know that coworker is going to be there, it seems to me you are absolutely justified in avoiding the work. On the other hand, you could ask this annoying coworker to leave. Perhaps you don't remember, but you invited him into your workspace once upon a time because you felt he would be helpful. You were younger then, and the work seemed more intimidating, and you wanted some help, that's all, because you must have thought it was important that you never make a mistake of any kind.

I think it's best that you ask him to leave. You will miss him in a way at first, because you have grown accustomed to his voice, and you will feel a bit alone, but that feeling quickly passes. You will love the new silence. Within it, you can hear yourself more clearly, which is why you were drawn to the work in the first place. You have always wanted to be alone with your work, and once you are, you will fully understand that the voice had never been you.

FEEL NO PAIN

AS I UNDERSTAND IT, women's inability to remember the pain of childbirth is evolutionary. The theory goes that if women *did* remember the pain of childbirth they would be far less likely to have a second baby, let alone a third, fourth, or fifth. Leave it to science to reduce humanity's capacity to endure suffering to some handy genetic blind spot. As if bringing forth life is akin to touching a hot stove.

And now, to think about it, while I have never given birth, I have had my share of physical pain, and the truth is I can't remember any of it. For instance, once during an aikido demonstration I rolled my ankle. I still remember the awareness that my foot was twisted the wrong way, I can remember the sound of my tendon popping, but I cannot actually remember the physical pain. I do remember rolling on the ground and clutching my ankle; I do remember, as if it were yesterday, how afraid I was that I wouldn't be able to work and support the child my wife was about to deliver—but I cannot remember the actual physical sensation.

Suspicious, isn't it? And isn't it odd how hollow our writing becomes when we try to describe pain? Isn't it odd how words like searing, burning, and aching fail to render this sensation we call pain. I read these words in a book and they are nothing but code to remind me that the character is in physical pain, but I feel nothing.

Yet the moment the writer renders fear, love, loss, or desire I am there with the character. It is almost as if physical pain means nothing at all, can leave no mark but the odd scar. It is as if all that actually matters to us is what we fear and what we love.

THE BRASS RING

THE ROGER WILLIAMS PARK ZOO in Providence, Rhode Island, used to have a merry-go-round equipped with a ring-grabbing game. Affixed to a post near the edge of the merry-go-round was a slender rectangular box loaded with metal rings. The box fed one ring at a time from a kind of lip, so that children riding the outermost horses could lean out and, if they timed it right, snatch the ring with a crooked finger. Most of the rings were black, but sometimes the box fed a brass-colored ring. If you were lucky enough to snatch this ring, you got a free ride. I always believed this was where the term "grab the brass ring" was derived.

I enjoyed this game. I found merry-go-rounds interesting for about two rotations, at which point I was done waving to my mother as she whirled past, and then there were the lions again, and there was the ice cream vendor again. But this little game brought purpose to going around in circles. I liked the feeling of leaning out from my horse, one hand tethering me to the pole, the other stretched and waiting, timing the rise and fall of my mount as the ring approached.

Even if I got a black ring I felt a sense of accomplishment, for if nothing else I was practicing for the big one.

And when it happened that I came around and the kid four horses in front of me snatched a black ring and out popped a brass, I thought, "Now's *my* time." I felt as if all eyes were on me, as if the whole park were pulling for me. Now I gathered myself, gathered all my attention to that ring and my waiting finger—and I had it! I'd done it! Which meant ... which meant getting back on the merry-go-round, and there was my mother waving, and there were the lions, and there was the ice cream vendor.

I have always been susceptible to reaching for brass rings. Oh, the thrill of winning, of being singled out, of acquiring specialness through achievement. It was a deceiving game, because I cared nothing for the ring or the ride but only for the grabbing—and even more than the grabbing, the trying to grab, the fundamental pleasure of harnessing my energy and attention. I would go looking for brass rings my whole life until I understood I was never supposed to grab it but to share it.

INFORMATION

THERE IS A LESSON ALL WRITERS COULD LEARN from scientists when it comes to results. For the scientist engaged in an experiment, all results are one thing and one thing only: information. In this way, the scientist's emotional detachment serves him or her well. The scientist is trained, theoretically, to be a disengaged observer, interested only in what the result of a given experiment can teach him or her, instead of a cheerleader for this or that outcome.

Writers, particularly once we move our work from our desk to the marketplace of other people's opinion, tend to lean toward the cheerleader. And for obvious reasons. The goal for all writers is the same: find those people with whom our work most resonates. These are the people who will represent it, publish it, and buy it. With all our attention trained on this one particular outcome, it is easy to reject the information contained within results we judge as unwanted.

It was Edison who said, of his first one hundred attempts at creating a light bulb, that he had not failed one hundred times, but had instead *succeeded* in finding one hundred ways *not* to make a light bulb. Sometimes this is true of rejection letters. Before the rejection letter, we did not know if this agent was the right agent; now we do. Information. Sometimes, however, rejection letters may tell us, in one way or another, that we need to rewrite our query letters; or that we need to submit to different types of agents; or that we need to rewrite our book. And of course sometimes letters tell us that we have found the right agent or publisher.

The world does not want you to fail. The world is forever supplying you with the information needed to do exactly what you want. Whether you accept this information or not is up to you. But do not fear the information. It is always friendly. The only thing to fear is your judgment of that information. When those letters come back, don your lab coat and pocket protector and look with friendly eyes upon what the world wishes you to know, and be grateful that you are one letter wiser.

Evolving Choice

I'VE ALWAYS HAD MIXED FEELINGS about the theory of evolution. Not the humans evolving from monkeys part. Everything clearly evolves. I evolve; you evolve; the birds, bees, bears, and baboons evolve. Once we huddled in caves, thrilled to light a fire; now we watch revolutions in Egypt on our iPhones. Every thought, every gesture, every printed book or hole in the ground changes the world irrevocably, for we cannot go back to the universe that existed before that hole was dug, the gesture made, the thought thought.

It was natural selection about which I had misgivings, because it suggested all of life evolved through a combination of random mutations and the irresistible compulsion of all living things—from amoebas to elephants—to make more of itself while avoiding death. Nowhere in any of this was that with which I have lived every day of my life: free choice.

To me this has always been the burden and the gift of consciousness. I can do anything, which is dizzying at times. I am *always* having to choose every single thing I do, say, and think. It is relentless. No one or thing has ever been able to choose anything for me. They have tried, but in the end I must still give my Yay or Nay before I take a single step. I don't know about squirrels and llamas, but for humans, life is one endless and contiguous stream of choices. Was evolution chosen or imposed? I don't know, but for my money, any theory that does not take into account free choice needs to be revisited.

And if I were to revisit the theory of evolution, I would begin with this question: Why does all life desire to live? What is the mathematical or alchemical formula that requires everything from dandelions to Barack Obama to live, live, live, live, and make more life that can go on living? And if everything in my life is a choice, is not that very act of living a choice as well?

Art has long sought to tackle this question. The question, after all, is like a joke that ceases to be funny once it is explained, just as our stories defy the tidy containment of a thesis paper or the ravings of a deconstructionist screed. No matter what you are writing, the answer that has eluded scientists forever lies within that urge to create what was not there before. We already know the answer, for we are living it, the meaning is always the act of choice itself.

Gift Of The Night

ONE EVENING WHEN I WAS ELEVEN, my younger brother, my older sister, my best friend Palmer, and I were looking for something to do. It was a windy, stormy Friday evening, dinner was done, and the world outside our windows looked brightly dark, the rain clear but the sky cloudy, the trees frantic in the wind. The night itself seemed alive and interesting. "Outside!" I said, and we donned our coats and made for the yard.

The wind beat in the trees, the clouds rushed east, but we were safe. We were privy to all the life of a storm without the threat. At first, this was enough. At first, merely being outside feeling both small and happy beneath the mighty night was enough. But then the bag appeared. It was a plastic Wonder Bread bag, dotted with circus colors, and it arrived on the wind out of the night, full as a sail, ghostly and alive as it flew east. The bag raced toward us, suspended over our heads like a fish on a stream of air. There was no question that when it dipped with the wind that we should try to catch it, and there was no question that when we did catch the bag it was cause for celebration.

That game was too fun to play just once. So one of us held the bag at one end of the yard and released it into the wind, and the other three had to stop it before it made it past the cherry tree. Again and again we played release and catch until I found four long sticks, and now we were tribesmen, and the bag our prey, and now we had to stake it with our spears in the night, the bag that came alive when given to the wind. We were free. We were not in the house doing dishes like my mother, we were not in our rooms doing homework, we were not locked in school: we were free to chase the current of pleasure wherever it led us.

So I always thought—until I started writing a daily column for an online magazine. Day after day, week after week, and then year after year I had to find something of interest to write about. The more I wrote, the more I understood that anything—a rainy day, a shower, a bad night's sleep—led to what had always interested me most, the intersection of creativity and everyday life. We weren't free that night because we didn't have to do dishes or homework, we were free because we were living the gift of play, the search for the current of pleasure in everything.

REAL HOPE

I HAVE DEVELOPED A GROWING DISTASTE for reality. A friend told me recently he believes in hope, but he also believes in reality. I do not like this reality he believes in if it stands somehow in opposition to hope. Though I suppose it's an understandable misperception. Reality is what is here now or what was here before. Hope, on the other hand, is entirely about what has not yet happened. That is, you cannot hope your turkey sandwich is a ham sandwich if it *is* a turkey sandwich, though you might hope your turkey could *become* a ham sandwich through the miracle of an opened fridge.

In this way, reality bores me. I can't do much with it, for it has already been done. Hope has always been more interesting, for it lights the inherent optimism of creation. Creativity is always a hopeful thing. It must be. What have we but hope for what does not exist, since we don't yet have the thing itself?

And anyway, good luck getting ten people to agree on reality. We may all be willing to call a tree a tree (if we all speak English), but we will likely not be willing to agree it is the most beautiful tree in the park. Reality is forever torn apart by perception, life's final arbiter.

All of which is a good thing. Who would want to be bound to a reality not their own? Even the most hardened realist, whatever he or she is, will admit that something new will come tomorrow, something born out of the unreadable fruit of the mind, something likely based on this supposed reality and yet ever so slightly beyond it. Hurrah for tomorrow. We cannot live for it, but it keeps us honest, keeps us from believing too firmly in today.

FORWARD

ALL SUFFERING, IT SEEMS TO ME, stems from one of two thoughts, both of which I have toiled under at one point or another in my work.

The first thought is, "I don't know what I want." Staring at the blank page of your day or your story or your life, you feel not the satisfying hum of a desire seeking its form, but the carcass of an idea. We follow many ideas that for one reason or another are stillborn within the womb of our imagination. This is a part of the experiment of life. Our pain comes when we mistake this single dead idea for our complete creative potential. Simply thinking the thought, "I don't know what I want,"—not with a story or a moment, but at *all*—cuts you off immediately from everything that will ever bring you pleasure. Just like your characters, you must always want something; it is as natural to you as breathing. That you are not hearing that desire is a measure of the noise of your mind, not the curiosity of your soul.

Which brings us to the second thought, "I know what I want, but I am incapable of having it." This is the song of the Broken You. I want love, but I am unlovable; I want to publish, but my work is unpublishable. By some cosmic toss of the die, you came up short. There's nothing to be done. You needed to be just a little bit better.

Your desires are always aligned with your abilities. Always. In fact, your abilities arise specifically and only to meet those desires. That you may need to acquire a few skills is irrelevant; humans are skill-acquiring machines. The delay between the desire and its fruition has everything to do with the quality of one's attention. It is as if we have a kind of psychic bank account. Every time we think, "I can," we put money in; and every time we think, "I can't," we take money out.

It is important to remember that just as it hurts to bend your finger backwards, so too will it hurt to think you cannot have what you want, or that there is nothing that you want. These thoughts run in complete contradiction to your nature. You were born wanting that next thing; your birth was your first expression of it here on earth. Go only forward; that is the direction of life.

WAITING FOR FREEDOM

WHEN I WAS A BOY, my family and I would join the sweaty throngs on the hillside overlooking Roger Williams Park Zoo amphitheater to watch a Rhode Island-sized fireworks display. This experience was divided into three distinct phases of waiting.

Because the fireworks could not begin until the canvas of the night sky was thoroughly black, and because one must arrive early to get a good position, there were hours of waiting between stretching out on your blanket and the first explosion. The only schedule was darkness, and so the waiting gradually acquired a speculative quality, the final moments being spent measuring the blackness of the overhead blue for its firework-worthiness.

Then, without any warning, something would happen. Oh, the relief! With a whistle and a crack and a shower of light, the waiting was over. Or it had changed. First, there was the brief, expectant wait between fireworks, filled with commentary on the relative extraordinariness of each display. But as the fireworks progressed, anticipation of the finale began to build, wondering with each new whistle if this would be another one-shot or the first of the coming frenzy. Finally it came, and the sky was filled with light upon light, your chest shaking with the thunder-crack of sound, everyone cheering, and the faces of your family and hillside neighbors glowing yellow, then red, then blue.

And then it was over. For a moment, silence. Then—the escape. Somehow, someone must have gotten out of that park quickly, but we were never one of those lucky few. Leaning against the backseat window, the night illuminated by headlights, I waited as we inched our way toward freedom, certain it would come, either by the roads my mother followed, or the sleep that would soon overtake me.

FEEL FIRST

ONCE WHILE SITTING IN A HOTEL BAR with some coworkers having a post shift cool-down I noticed a woman sitting across the bar by herself. She was dressed strangely alluringly, and she kept looking up from her drink as if she were looking for someone. Not *expecting* someone, but looking for someone. Eventually her eyes landed on me, and I understood that she was a prostitute and that I was being sized up as a potential client. This is a look not unlike you would receive from a vendor in a mall kiosk to determine if you might want a hair de-curler or foot salt, only more predatory.

Once she had concluded I was not a possible customer and her attention wandered elsewhere, I nudged one of my coworkers and told her about the prostitute because I guess I was just that unworldly that I had to tell somebody.

"So?" said my friend. "Maybe you should take her up on it?"

"One, I'm married; and two—no. It would be awful."

"Why? It's just sex? Why would it be so awful?"

I can't remember what I said at the time, but it was unconvincing; I ended up sounding vaguely like a televangelist. I'm sure my friend pitied my wife for having married such an uptight rube. It was not until recently that I understood why it would have been such a bad idea for me, whether I was married or not.

If I had hired the woman, I would have done so for one of two reasons: either because I believed I was not worthy enough for a woman to be with me unless I paid her or because I *wanted* to pay her, because I felt women had too much control over the mating dance and this was my only way of gaining control back. Or some other reason, but these will do. The point is, in order to go through with the act, I would have to believe one of these unhappy stories. In fact, I would have to maintain the story and the feelings it engendered from proposition to payment or else I would lose the desire, because the desire was based upon the feeling of the story.

In other words, I would have to consciously make myself feel bad in order to do it. Sometimes it seems as though we already feel bad, so we act from this bad feeling, and there we are with a table full of coke or a hotel prostitute. But in truth, we maintain the story all along the way. If we did not keep telling the story, we would lose the energy for whatever we were doing.

Which is why one of my rules of writing is: feel first, write second. But feel what you *want* first, and then find the story to fit it. You can tell yourself any story you want, just as you can choose any book in a bookstore. You might as well pick the one that makes you happiest.

THE GOOD DOCTOR

MY PARENTS DIVORCED WHEN I WAS SEVEN, leaving me, technically, as the man of the house. By which I mean John, my younger brother, instinctively turned to me for guidance that would have otherwise been provided by our father. I think that for many years I resented this role and so was not a particularly gracious big brother. I was also fiercely competitive, and I was not going to allow John to be better than me at anything, which for a time he dutifully wasn't. We eventually became quite close, and when I look back I believe this closeness started with the arrival of Dr. VonVickenvoctor.

Doctor, as we usually called him, was a purple muppet to which we had adhered two button eyes and a mustache made of yarn. I may have been moody and competitive, but I loved to be entertained, and one day John, age ten, sat down on the couch across from me and introduced me to Doctor.

What followed was the first of many shows. Doctor—a greedy, libidinous, self-absorbed billionaire—would tell me about the time he ... and then the story. Doctor could travel at will through time and space, and wherever he went, things always went askew. No matter, Doctor always came back for more, never changing, never learning, a purple ego muttering, "Me ... me ... me ..." as he considered his next bizarre plan.

I loved him. My brother had a genius for improvisation and puppetry, and for the duration of those shows I became an eager audience, in the process handing the wheel of our friendship to my little brother. Doctor told me stories for years, and things between John and me grew steadily better.

John would go on to be an actor/writer/director, and at my wedding he gave a moving speech, during which he spoke about how I had been a kind of creative mentor to him. I have always had lots to say about writing and stories and the arts in general, and no doubt John was made to listen to much of it, but I believe in retrospect my gift to his artistic development was not my lectures and diatribes, but those puppet shows.

In entertaining me he must have glimpsed in me, the ferocious big brother, the power of laughter and of joy and his own capacity to harness that power. Talking is fine, but listening is always the greatest gift. Within the attentive audience's perched silence the artist often hears his voice clearly for the first time. Your mind, after all, was given so you could talk to yourself; but your voice you were given to talk to others.

HISTORY IN THE FLESH

I INTERVIEWED THE HISTORICAL NOVELIST Margaret George shortly after she had released *Elizabeth I*, a book that includes an intimate portrait of not just the queen and her many courtiers and ladies, but also William Shakespeare—whose appearance, I have to admit, had me sitting up a little straighter in my reading chair. Silly, I know, because it was only George's imagining of The Bard, but still—my disbelief was fully suspended. I wanted to meet the man.

Sometimes you go in search of history, and sometimes it sits down and talks to you. Three days before I met Margaret George, I spoke with Caroline Kennedy about *She Walks in Beauty*, a collection of poems that had inspired her over her lifetime. I did not intend to talk about her family, but for Kennedy, poetry and her family are inextricable. So there we were talking about her mother and father, and I had to remind myself exactly whom she meant.

It was history in the flesh—only it wasn't, because John and Jacqueline were just her parents, and John-John was just her brother, just like Shakespeare was just a writer. I thought of Kennedy when I was chatting with Margaret George after our interview, and she mentioned something she'd heard Sylvester Stallone say: "We all invent our own mythology."

I couldn't agree more. Kennedy said she authored her first anthology, *The Best-Loved Poems of Jacqueline Kennedy Onassis*, after her mother's death, when the public seemed fixated almost entirely upon Onassis's fashion sense. She was trying, however vainly, to rewrite the evolving Jackie O mythology.

Shortly after talking to Kennedy, a man in the bookstore asked what I had been doing. I told him. He shook his head in wonder. "What a woman," he said. "So grounded. What a national treasure." As he said this, his eyes seemed to be focused somewhere far off, on some mountaintop where the national treasures reside. There they must stay, if we aim to be inspired by their perfection. Or, if we choose, we could join them by standing perfectly still, surrounded entirely by history forever in the making.

THE WICKED AMONG US

I HAVE HAD THREE STEPMOTHERS in my life, although I don't know if your father's wives are truly stepmothers if you've never lived with them. Still, three stepmothers are satisfyingly fairytale-ish, which serves this story. I did live for a short time with one of these women–the first, when I was eight. My brother, sister, and I spent a month in Florida with my father and his new wife, Eloise. I didn't get along with Eloise. She made me eat everything on my plate, and I was a very picky eater. At one point, she forced me to eat mashed potatoes until I threw up. She then made me keep eating them.

During this trip we rented a camper and visited Disney World. Early on, I made the observation to Eloise that, "Isn't it funny that here we are in Disney World, and you're like the evil stepmother?"

Later that evening my father took me for a walk. He said I needed to apologize to Eloise. "Why?" I asked. He mentioned the evil step-mother comment. I was honestly confused. If a woman who makes you keep eating mashed potatoes after eating mashed potatoes induces vomiting isn't evil, then who is? I don't remember how the rest of the discussion went, but I wound up apologizing to Eloise. She sat me on her lap and delivered a long lecture about respect and love–I think. I didn't listen.

My father left Eloise shortly after this and returned to Providence to live closer to his children. As far as I know, the mashed potatoes incident did not factor into the move. I do remember that for Christmas I sent him a framed school photo of myself. The story goes that he opened my gift Christmas morning, began to cry, and that was the end of his second marriage.

Eloise has always made a very convenient villain in the story of my life. I refused to eat mashed potatoes for the next thirty-five years. If anyone questioned my feelings about mashed potatoes, I would happily tell them my Florida story. It was my badge of suffering.

And then a few years ago, at the Pacific Northwest Writers Conference, I was served a dinner of filet mignon and garlic mashed potatoes. It had been a long day at the conference, and I was hungry. What's more, I had recently started a magazine, I was meeting all kinds of wonderful writers, and I was no longer waiting tables. I turned to my wife. "I'm going to eat them."

I took a bite. They were quite delicious. So I finished the whole plate, and the wicked queen was dead.

YOUR ONLY VICTORY

CHRISTOPHER MOORE SAID that writer's block is giving fear a name. Strange in a way, this distinction, for doesn't fear already have a name, and isn't that name: Fear? Yes, but how effective would it be were it left so naked? Best to dress it up, give it a role and a title, and then it isn't merely *fear*, some hobgoblin of an idea we can dismiss— now it is Something Real. Now fear is a person or a disease or worse yet, a Fact, and so we must deconstruct it, disprove it, defeat it.

And as soon as we attempt any of these, we have lost. You cannot disprove fear any more than you can prove love. But fear invites you to disprove it, requires it even, for in your struggle fear grows stronger, because the more you try and the more you fail to disprove fear, the more real fear becomes. After all, why would you bother trying to disprove if it weren't real? Your very efforts prove its reality, and the more you struggle to answer a question that you alone asked, the further into the forest of this nightmare you wander.

When I look into this mirror we call writing, I see all of life reflected back at me. Nothing I have ever done in my life has ever filled me with so much fear or made me so happy. I wish sometimes, like a child alone in a dark house for the first time, that some wiser presence would come home and turn on all the lights for me. Yet if it were to be so, I would be no safer, for only time would separate me from the fear waiting to answer the call of my own thoughts.

Writing means so much to me precisely because I have so feared it. As it is nothing to love your brother but everything to love your enemy, so too is it true that you learn the most in the moment when you at last understand that the monster is you. Fear deserves no name but your own, for it was never more than an idea of yours in the first place, and what we call victory is actually surrender.

THE WINDOW OF YOU

ANDRE DUBUS III POINTED OUT that when you write you must let go of your Self. But aren't we writing to reveal and express the Self? Isn't the Self that which distinguishes us from all the other Selves on the planet?

Indeed it is, but imagine for a moment the difference between the windowpane and the window frame. The frame is the bracket that defines the space that is the window and holds the pane that allows light into the room. Without the frame, there can be no window, and without a window, there can be no light.

But wait: of course there is light without the window, it just hasn't found its way into the room. The light was always there—it existed before the window was cut and will shine on long after the window has been boarded up tight. When we cut a hole in a wall we are grateful for the frame that shapes the light, but it is the light we are seeking first and always.

You are both the frame and the pane, and your objective is to be that open space through which light might shine. When we begin to become enamored of our shape, our defined selves, the light begins to dim. It is as if we have taken that light that was meant to shine through us and refracted it back on our forms.

It is the same light that shines through all of us, we are merely positioned at different points in the universe, and so the light comes through shaped and shaded slightly differently. This is why we can best celebrate that which is us by forgetting that which defines us. That frame, that shape, can do nothing, can warm nothing, can illuminate nothing—but the light it permits is what life actually looks like.

INTERESTING DIRECTION

A LOT OF NOVELS, both published an unpublished, are populated by a recurring character: the Fantasy Love Interest.

You have a novel filled with interesting, rounded people, and then along comes the Love Interest, whose only real flaw is that he or she is not yet paying full attention to our protagonist. The Love Interest reminds me of how someone eager to be in a relationship might describe a prospective mate after two dates that went reasonably well, sanitized to maintain the fantasy.

But this is how we are. We have two parts: the one desperate to be loved and the other that simply loves. The part that wants to be loved doesn't really love anything, it just wants attention so that it is certain it is worthy of love. The part that loves, however, loves life itself, and life is always a direction. When we love someone, we love their direction, not their attention.

I wasted many, many, many hours of my life craving this or that girl's or woman's attention. In these wasted hours, the objects of my desire were kept suspended in a cartoon world, beautiful blank slates who might one day turn my way, and in their eyes I would come alive as I finally saw myself. And then I met my wife, and there I was and always had been—not in her eyes, but looking out from within, chasing the direction that interested me most.

A LOSING FORMULA

IN THE LATE 1970S, my father brought home a strategy football game. The game was quite simple. Whoever was on defense had a deck of cards, each with a different defensive alignment. The game's board was a grid, along the top of which were twenty or so different offensive plays, from Dive to Razzle Dazzle (my brother's favorite). The defenses ran along the side. The player on offense would announce which play he was running and the player on defense would reveal which alignment he had selected, the two choices would be cross-referenced like finding coordinates on an X-Y plane, and you would learn the result of that play.

In this way, it was really a guessing game, not a strategy game. It became an intuitive, psychological struggle to read the other player's mind and proclivities. There was a lot of, "He thinks I'll throw a bomb, but I'll actually run a dive–unless he thinks I think he thinks I'll run a dive, in which case I'll throw the bomb." You were always better off going with your first instinct.

At this time, my father had begun to learn how to program computers. He looked at this game and began to hatch a scheme. He believed he could come up with a program that would tell which play or defense would have the highest rate of success given the down, distance, and so on. He dreamt of having his children go to a big gaming tournament armed with a stack of computer printouts and whipping all the adult competitors.

Fortunately, the permutations proved too expansive for either my father's know-how or actual interest in the project. I believe it was probably the latter. It seemed emblematic of his struggle at that time: a doomed search for a means by which the straight line of intellect could triumph over the reasonless nudge of intuition.

I was glad to see this plan die. My heart always sank when he painted the image of our theoretical triumph. On the one hand he was my father, and he had so many dreams; it would have been nice to have just one *not* come up well short of where he imagined it might take him. On the other hand, intuition seemed like the great equalizer in human endeavor, available to all regardless of age or income. Why look to triumph over it?

I cannot blame him for wanting a world that could be won with computer programs. Like all fathers, he wanted his children to be safe, and I do not believe he understood where safety could be found outside the clear perimeters of logic. But where is the safety in a life stripped of choice? That safety is a seed still buried, hiding beneath a world where anything is possible.

THE HERD

WRITERS SOMETIMES MAKE RELUCTANT CAPITALISTS, but whether we wish to discuss it or not, we are responsible for creating a product that we must in turn sell to the general public. The knock on capitalism, generally speaking, is its coldheartedness, a necessarily unfeeling engine of commerce whose deity, The Market, rights all wrongs through a Darwinian winnowing of the entrepreneurial herd. We writers, meanwhile, usually like to view ourselves as caring, empathetic people. Empathy is more or less in the fiction writer's job description; How else to render believably all those people who aren't us?

But there is something beautifully democratic about capitalism that every business owner, including writers, at some point understands. We all have our own crowd. We all have the people we eat and drink with, the people we seek out at parties. Society, in some ways, remains an extension of the high school cafeteria, with everyone gravitating to their respective tables. It's not always inspiring, but it's practical; easier to talk to people you like than to those you don't.

But then you become a writer, and someone from another lunch table does something unexpected: they buy your book. In fact, you might look up to realize that *only* people from other lunch tables are buying your book. Now these people aren't so bad after all. And not merely because they're putting quarters in your pocket. When you meet your readers you discover for whom, beside yourself, you were actually writing.

Though I was the sort who bounced between different lunch tables, I have my preferences. While it is gratifying in a way to learn that someone I know and perhaps admire likes my work, there is something singularly uplifting about a stranger finding comfort in it. On the savannah, herd animals seek safety in numbers. Writers must go it alone to do our work, and our safety, in the end, depends on our willingness to accept all comers, to welcome round us anyone whose questions match our own. You see life then for what it is: a collection of curiosity, whose form must yield by and by to the answers received.

KING FOR A NIGHT

THE LEGEND OF BEETHOVEN'S *Ninth Symphony* goes as follows: the composer, already stone deaf, was commissioned by The Philharmonic Society of London, and, after six years of composing, produced the symphony, which premiered in 1824 at the Kärntnertor theater in Vienna. According to witnesses, at the symphony's conclusion, Beethoven received five standing ovations. The king only got three, and so the police were forced to break up the proceedings.

As an artist I take a certain glee in this story, whether it is true or not. How delightful that the composer, who was unable to marry the woman he loved because she was of noble birth and he was not, in the end produced something so beautiful it broke the laws of class divide. How delicious that the audience was compelled to reward accomplishment over blood.

But how much more beautiful this other anecdote, that the conductor left his podium to turn to Beethoven, who sat in a chair to the side of musicians, so that he could see the applause he could not hear. Beethoven had said of the *Ninth Symphony* and its climactic

"Ode to Joy" that he wished to give something great to humanity. Yet he was forced to do so while condemned to silence, kept not only from the applause it inspired but from the music itself.

And so there was the *Ninth Symphony* heard by the audience that day in Vienna, and the *Ninth Symphony* heard by Beethoven alone, the one played in the concert hall of his imagination. Looking out into that sea of silent applause, it must have seemed an odd and fitting end to a musical career. Let the same silence needed to compose the Ode reply to its debut. He gave love in silence and received it so.

We put kings in castles, clothe and feed them, arm their guards, and put a pointed crown on their heads so that they might be closer to God, from whom they are now expected to receive instruction for the greater good, unburdened as they are by earthly concerns. But the needs of the flesh can be sated or, in Beethoven's case, abandoned by necessity–no matter, you return to the soul by either route, and a little wooden chair on the edge of a stage could stand as high as a throne.

A SIMPLE TEST

WHEN I WAS SEVENTEEN my father convinced me to take a career aptitude test. This was a 2-hour, multiple-choice questionnaire from whose answers a qualified professional would be able to determine what sort of work I should pursue. I didn't want to take the test. I already knew what I wanted to do. I wanted to write. I knew this because when I asked myself, "What do you want to do, Bill?" I always answered, "Write." That was my short version of this test.

Plus, I didn't like what this test insinuated. I did not like that some test held the answer to such an important question, a question I was for some reason unequipped to answer alone. What if all those dots I filled in added up to engineer or accountant? Writing had enough confidence pitfalls built-in, did I really need more? In the back of my mind was something a teacher had recently said. This teacher had known me since I was a freshman, knew me as well as any teacher in my high school. She told me that when she watched me solving math problems, I seemed more focused than when I was doing any other kind of work, including writing. She wondered if I had thought of going into accounting. Her husband, by the way, was an accountant.

I took the test. For two hours I replied that I would rather read a book than build a model train, that I preferred English classes to Math classes. When I was done I told my father I thought the test was stupid, that I already knew what I wanted to do. He told me to wait and see. A week later I had my meeting with the qualified professional. The qualified professional told me that based upon the results of the test I might want to consider a career that involved writing in some form or another. I told him I planned to be a writer. He said, "That should work."

My father was mildly disappointed. I think he believed my desire to write was some bohemian fantasy. But the test had spoken, so he wasn't about to argue. I may have been a little smug coming out of the qualified professional's office that afternoon. But wouldn't it have been even better if the test *had* come back engineer? Wouldn't it have been better to have gone ahead without the hollow backing of some silly test? It was a nice "I told you so," but no test score could prop me up when the rejection letters trickled in. Then I had to take my own test again. Then I had to ask myself, "What do you want to do, Bill?" And again the answer was, "Write."

I DON'T KNOW WHY

I KNEW A MAN ONCE who refused to answer "why questions." The way he said it always irritated my inner snark, and I was sorely tempted to ask, "And why is that?"

But the truth is, he had a point. Why questions are ultimately unanswerable. I am not talking about certain factual why questions, like, "Why is the sky blue?" or, "Why do helium balloons float?" Rather, I am speaking now of the personal why questions, like, "Why do you like blue cheese?" or, "Why do you write?" The only reason we do anything is because we like to do it or we think we might like to do it, and the only reason we like anything is because we like it.

My friend's problem–or, I should say *my* problem with my friend–was that his refusal to answer the why questions was phrased with almost political defiance, as if he were on the witness stand pleading the fifth. But again, this is understandable. Whenever I ask myself, "Why did you do that?" I really mean, more or less, "How could you have made such a mistake?" I never ask myself why I did something when the results turn out sparkling.

Much of the job of fiction writers is to probe why their characters do what they do. Most of our characters get into trouble, but they do so with the belief that their actions will bring them happiness or at least relief from misery. We often understand our characters not as an engineer understands the physics of a skyscraper, but as a friend understands another friend–sympathetically–recognizing in ourselves the same doubt and anguish that led us to entanglements from which we had to eventually free ourselves–the stuff of good fiction.

I believe despair waits for us at the very end of every why question because the question assumes an architectural order to the universe that does not exist. Everything architectural is by necessity static, while life remains perpetually in motion. When we ask why, we are really begging to see this false order revealed so that we might stand at last on firm ground and feel safe. When the order does not emerge, we are left believing that either we are incapable of finding it, and so we have failed, or that the universe is built on sand, and safety is impossible.

The question we really want to ask of ourselves is never "Why?" but "What?" What do I most want at this moment? This we can know, and every time we answer it we learn again that it was never safety we were seeking but happiness.

LOOK NEW

IF RULE ONE FOR MOST WRITERS is, "Show don't tell," then rule two is probably, "Never use clichés!" The exclamation point is mine–because although I would never argue with either of these rules, it seems to me that rule two is our most punishable offense, the schoolmarm's knuckle-cracking yardstick of writing wisdom.

I don't believe in doing anything to avoid punishment. This to me is a backward way to go about things, since life, whether we like it or not, is always led toward and never away from. So let's take another, more compassionate look at clichés and why our work is always better served without them.

All clichés worked once. One of my favorite clichés is, "The silence was deafening." Isn't that lovely? And quite deft, using the oxymoronic "deafening" to compel the reader to re-imagine overwhelming silence. The problem for writers is not that someone has already used this phrase and by doing so yourself you are committing the shameful sin of unoriginality; rather, by using this cliché you are denying your reader the opportunity to see the world anew.

Whatever your readers pictured in their mind's eye when they first read a cliché like the one above will remain with them forever, to be regurgitated whenever those words appear on a page. Whatever it is you are looking to describe cannot possibly be the very same thing your readers were having described to them when they created their mental image, and yet that is what they will see.

If you write to avoid shame, all your efforts are, in the end, selfish in the very worst sense of that word. There is no satisfaction in selfishness; selfishness satisfied is only fear delayed. But when you write generously, you write toward the gift and not away from the shame. Your gift is vision, to see clearly what has always been directly before us, and in so doing remind the reader, and yourself, that every silence and every flower and every person defies the confines of a single idea.

LIFE IN TRANSLATION

I AM NOT ONE OF THOSE PEOPLE who find a medium's lack of specificity unconvincing. On the contrary, I think I would be more skeptical if a medium could take one look at a subject and describe every dead relative in one go.

The times I have heard mediums attempting to communicate with the dead, I am always reminded of my own efforts to write a story. When I write I feel as though I am listening, not making, and this listening begins with vague images that interest me and upon which I then focus until the images become clearer and lead to other images.

I think the listening distinction is important because it takes the pressure off the writer. You must enter a relaxed state to listen. You must shut your mind down and wait for whatever it is you are listening for to speak. This makes writing a less formidable task. You don't have to make everything up from nothing; you only have to hone your skills as a translator.

I know there are charlatans all about us, and I cannot say precisely what mediums see and hear when they are talking to the dead, but I know they see and hear something, because we all do. Everyone who has ever written a story or painted a picture or started a business or changed careers uses much the same language: "The idea came to me." And indeed it does. The ideas always come to us; we don't go get them. Everyone's life, after all, is a story being told in the present tense. Everyone is listening to suggestions and translating them into actions—into dinners and movies and families and stories alike. But nothing can come to you if you don't listen, and nothing heard can be built upon if you aren't patient. Like the mediums asking questions of their subject, we are all tuning and tuning the frequency of our interest, and as we do, we come to understand that strange paradox, that we must grow increasingly still to receive the information needed to move us forward.

THE LIVING

MIDWAY THROUGH MY SENIOR YEAR in high school, our principal dropped dead of a heart attack. I was the co-editor of the yearbook, and it was decided we would dedicate our edition to him, even though Mr. McCarthy, our principal, had been a strangely out-of-place man, a mild-mannered, tweed jacket-wearing WASP, overseeing a largely black and Hispanic student body, who drifted quietly through the halls not bothering us as long as we didn't bother him. Still, our previous principal had been imprisoned for insurance fraud, so he was a step in the right direction. Until he died.

It was also decided that I should present his widow with a special copy of the yearbook at our graduation and that I should say something in honor of this somber occasion. I wrote words to the effect of, "So many of the names of the faces in the yearbook would be forgotten over time, but no one would ever forget Mr. McCarthy." I don't know if this would have been true if he hadn't died, but I couldn't think of anything else to say.

And so it was that I found myself standing on stage behind a podium before the entire graduating class and all their available relatives, when not three words into my little speech my graduation cap slipped from my head and fell to the stage. Apparently I said, "Oops," quite loudly into the microphone, which inspired a big, relieved laugh from the auditorium. From the darkened seats beneath me I heard one of my track teammates call out, "That's all right, Bill!"

And it was. The whole thing went quite smoothly after that, and when I was done I ceremoniously handed the engraved copy to Mrs. McCarthy, a small shy woman who seemed sort of dazed, as if she were still learning what life was like without Mr. McCarthy to go home to. She appeared quite touched by our gesture, which depressed me a little—but what could be done? None of us had wished him dead, and we were all trying to make the best of it, and now it was time to graduate and begin the rest of our young lives.

I think everyone was grateful that cap fell off my head when it did, even Mrs. McCarthy. Before that moment, the ceremony was in danger of becoming a dry reflection of our own stiff and uncertain relationship with death. But then life popped through, and everyone breathed, and we were allowed to enjoy ourselves again, because life still belonged to the living.

THE LONELY DESPOT

IF I WERE AN AMBITIOUS DESPOT, I would spend most of my hours concerned about free will. Even if I put my subjects in chains, whipped them, and put guns to their heads, the fact that these tortured and threatened subjects would still be able to think and believe anything they wished would keep me up at night. Every insurrection begins as an idea. One idea begets another idea, and then another idea, until one such idea is so attractive that someone acts. What to do, what to do, what to do?

I am sure I would learn the secret all despots come to know: that humans are limited in their desire, that not everyone can be attracted to all things equally, but that humans *can* be afraid of anything. And since I cannot control what my subjects love, I would try to suggest what they should fear. Fortunately for me, the despot, the future is unknown. I must keep this future a frightening and dangerous place, a place in which they cannot hope to be safe without my vigilance, without my firm omnipotent control.

Yet even if I were a very skilled despot, even if I had a vast and loyal secret police, trained and enthusiastic in the practice of intimidation, even if my subjects spied on one another, distrusted one another, there would still be many nights I would lie awake concerned about the limits of my influence. Being such an expert on the matter, I would know that fear is only a distraction, as if I had set off a terrifying fireworks display upon which all their eyes were now trained. How do you keep their eyes upon it? What if just one person turns away and sees I have no clothes?

If I were a despot, I would lie awake wondering, perhaps, how it was possible that I in my palace surrounded by my guards was as capable of fear as the lowest urchin? I would wonder if my subjects could believe this. I would wonder if they learned of their dear leader's fear, would they love me, and not just fear me. But then I would remember that I cannot control what anyone loves, and I would feel their rejection of me, and I would hate this rejection and how small and vulnerable and ugly it made me feel, and I would close my eyes and return to the nightmare of fear.

FRIENDLY DARK

I HAVE HEARD IT SAID that, "Just as darkness is the absence of light, evil is the absence of God." Interesting analogy, especially when we remember that in the Old Testament God's first act of creation is the introduction of light into the dark and shapeless void that was the universe.

The difference between the blank page and the shapeless void is only that of color and dimension. First there is always nothing. And then into this nothing there comes a word, and the writer sees that it is good. The page does not create the word, it merely receives it. Likewise, the blank page has nothing to say one way or another about which words are written on it. The blank page is as pristinely indifferent to language, to ideas, to stories, as the wood from which it was pounded. And yet it is this very indifference that makes it the perfect platform for creation.

Writer's block can look like indifference: the writer is stripped of interest, and, indifferent to her creations, can find no words to continue them. But writer's block is really fear of indifference and of the freedom it bestows. Writer's block is the recognition that *anything* is permissible, that the blank page provides no guidelines whatsoever, that nothing at all is inherently good or bad—all creation is equal except within the eyes of the creator.

If a serpent were to visit me at my desk, he would no doubt whisper about perfection. He would whisper that all creation cannot be equal, for look at the bestseller list. Look at the facts! And as he whispered, my attention might move from the light within me toward the darkness, as if I might try to understand darkness; solve it; defeat it. In this way, the serpent makes an enemy of a friend, that which in truth waits without judgment for the first spark of interest.

RATS AND BONES

I HAVE HAD TO MAKE PEACE with the unavoidable reality that I am an optimist. This was more challenging than you might think. Growing up, my two literary heroes were T. S. Elliot and Ernest Hemingway. When Prufrock asked, *"Do I dare disturb the universe? In a minute there are times for decisions and revisions which a minute will reverse,"* I felt he was speaking for me; and when Fredric Henry walks back to his hotel "in the rain," after his beloved Catherine dies delivering their stillborn child, I thought I had read one of the greatest endings in literature.

But I was a young man then, and I was deeply moved by anyone capable of peeling back the layer of everyday life to unearth the roots of our collective despair. Despair, after all, seemed to me to be everywhere; despair was the hobgoblin beneath every bed, the villain lurking in every shadowy street corner. If we reveal the beast, perhaps then we might slay him. This, I believed, was the writer's job, his (my) highest calling. Anything else was avoiding the truth, capitulating to the silent denial that was otherwise all around me.

Yet the silent truth turned out to be more generous than I had at first understood. When I was a freshman in college, we studied "The Waste Land." Of all the poems in Western Literature's canon, none cries out for teaching more than "The Waste Land." In a way, it is a literature professor's dream, so packed as it is with references and clues as to make it virtually opaque to the unschooled reader.

I was captivated. As the professor walked us through Dante and the quest for the grail, I felt as if life itself were being shown to me. That life was a wasteland did not bother me at all. In fact, weeks later the subject of the poem came up during a history class. I felt compelled to say of "The Waste Land," "It's strangely uplifting."

The professor looked at me blankly and asked, "Why?"

I couldn't answer. The full reply was too large for my eighteen-year-old heart, yet it was this: if we are despairing, there must be something worth despairing over. What all the rats and bones literature was really pointing me toward—whether the writers intended it or not—was that which they seemed to have lost. I was strangely uplifted because I understood I had a job to do. It was an important job, and that's all I wanted from life.

I became an optimist the day I found what I was looking for, exactly where I had left it, years before.

FAILED REVOLUTION

I FIND IT A LITTLE IRONIC that rational thinking, the golden child of The Enlightenment, became a kind of godfather of democracy. After all, it was rational thinking—logic and proof—that said you could be right not because you were the king or the pope but because you could demonstrate a truth based upon known facts. Just like that, we were on our way from a monarchy to a meritocracy, where we would be judged by our deeds and not our birth. The polls are open!

I find this ironic because one of the great lessons freedom teaches us is that we should pursue our own happiness, and that happiness has no logic whatsoever. Just ask a writer. Why does someone like a story? *Because he likes it.* Why does someone write a story? *Because she wants to write it.* You can talk about tension, or romance, or humor, but in the end you write what you write because you want to write it, and you read what you read because you want to read it. The reasons end there.

Very unsatisfying in a way. After all, we clawed our way to this freedom place by the power of reason only to find we have a little king or queen within us whose only explanation for why we should do something is, "Because I said so!" Where's the freedom in that? We could try rebelling. We could summon our Minute Men of Reason and say, "I will write based upon the market, for I want to make money because I need money to eat and live, and so I will look at the known facts, and that is what I will do because I am rational."

This revolution is doomed to fail. Your victory will be short lived. You will wind up a kind of dictator, filling your empire with Rules for Success, because rules are rational, and if you follow them, you will succeed and be safe. And when you don't succeed, you will make new rules, or scrap all the old ones and find new ones. And when you still don't succeed, you will blame the rest of world that is conspiring against you and your kindly regime.

We should always have compassion for kings and queens. Monarchy was our idea to begin with, after all. At some point, we all obey what we don't understand. At some point, we all kneel down to love, whose wisdom, we are happy to discover, defies all reason.

WHAT DREAMS MAY COME

I WAS TIRED because I had watched a television show the night before that involved too many people being stabbed and tortured. And so, as always happens to me, I spent the night dreaming of stabbings and torture and then awoke in the middle of the night, my brain darting from one faceless anxiety to the next, until I reminded myself no one that I knew was planning to stab and torture me, and I fell back asleep.

I went through a period in my late teens where I would dream often of my own impending execution. It so happened that these dreams coincided with the realization that I was not in fact immortal. This was sobering at the time, and seemed worthy of many stories and poems, but I have since decided that as a writer you are better served, at least during your writing, if you can hold a dispassionate view of death.

I thought of this again the other day as I was trying to come up with an appropriate curse to lay on one my characters. As I considered my choices, I realized that death, as a narrative threat, was not nearly as compelling as a character living their life knowing, say, that they would never love another.

We are often taught to believe that death is the worst thing that could happen to us, and so logically, to our characters as well. But all stories are told because the characters in them are seeking to change and to learn. Death, opaque as it may be, is a change. With it, the characters are released from whatever evils they had committed, whatever lies they had believed.

Far worse is a life without growth. This is the jail we all fear. When I tossed about in my bed, I wasn't actually afraid of being tortured and killed. Instead, I was staring down that timeless fear that all I am is a sack of meat that must be kept fed and clothed until the clock runs out. That is the promise of the slave driver's whip—that you can be driven from here to there by the needs of your body, not the yearning of your soul.

THE AUTHENTIC ENGINE

A FRIEND OF MINE ONCE ASKED ME where I come up with ideas for my stories. My explanation was that I might take my childhood house in Providence, put it in Los Angeles, and populate it with people I met in college in New York. "Oh," he said. "So it's like a dream."

"Exactly," I replied. A dream is perhaps the best and quickest description of the writing process. After all, aren't many stories begun in that fertile, idle state we call a "day dream?" However, I am as likely as not to ignore my sleeping dreams, which, like most people's, are abstract, surreal, and periodically repetitive and unsatisfying. I hope they've done their work, because once I'm out of bed, I'm on to other things.

But I have never doubted that dreams are important. And of course they are. Without dreams human beings go mad. Think about that for a moment: you literally *must* dream. These fragmented, Frankenstein narratives we call dreams are in a way more important than the sleep in which they are born. The deep rest of sleep is nothing more than a vehicle for spontaneous imagining.

Or, as any writer knows, re-imagining. For everything we write, everything we dream, is culled from all that we have done and known. Culled, and then rearranged into a new reality. The imagination is not interested in what is. What we call reality is merely the building material of the imagination, which knows only the vast and ever-shifting landscape of its own reality.

That our visions of our futures are called dreams is no linguistic coincidence. As you imagine yourself forward through time, you are rearranging in your imagination what has been to shape what will be. For this reason, the imagination loves the future, it is its playground, and the imagination is fearless when facing the future because it cannot be wrong. And this great tool with which everyone was gifted is not just a muscle for writing stories or painting pictures, it is the authentic engine that drives the human animal forward.

A QUESTION FOR YOU

I HAVE INTERVIEWED MANY different types of writers, and for every type of writer there is a different type of interview, but with every writer one thing remains consistent: the person matches the book. This is not to say that the writer and his or her work are one in the same. Instead, it's as if the writer is in a life-long discussion with the world, and a book is one part of that discussion. When I meet the writer, I feel that discussion still in process, as though the writer has asked a question of the world, and the answer is coming and coming and coming.

This is particularly helpful when I read books about which I am not excited. It is easy to feel that somehow the writer has set out to waste my time. But this is only because when I read a book, I am hearing it in my own voice. If the writer is posing a question which I have already answered to my own satisfaction or am simply not interested in asking myself, then what I hear in my head sounds like a song played in the wrong key.

On the other hand, once I meet the writers, and hear their voice, the question the book posed makes perfect sense—for that writer. It's then I realize that what bothered me most was the dissonance between my voice and that of the author's, not whether the book was any good or not.

It is impossible for me, once I meet someone, not to feel the integrity of that person's life question. Not the integrity of their answers, for none of them are ever meant to be final, only guideposts—but the question. That is the tension of life, just as it is the tension of fiction. But it is a dynamic tension, a creative tension, and it does not matter how far from my own question the dramatic arc of another person's life is drawn—it bends as necessarily and unstoppably forward as mine. I see this, and I am relieved. I am relieved as I am once again reminded that nothing in life can be gotten wrong, that the question is pure, and the answers are nothing more than cobblestones in the road you are paving in its pursuit.

THE PRIME MOVER

I OFFICIALLY STUDIED PHILOSOPHY for the first time during my freshman year in college. By "study philosophy" I mean I read works by philosophers, listened to philosophy professors explain the works of these philosophers, and then took tests and wrote papers demonstrating that I understood what I had read and what the professor had explained.

Not long into my studies of the Great Western Philosophers I thought to myself, *I can do that*. All philosophers do is look around at the world, reflect on what they see, and write down what they believe to be the truth about what they have perceived. Why spend all this time reading the conclusions other people have drawn when you are just as capable of drawing them yourself?

One of those philosophers I studied was Aristotle. I liked Aristotle. It seemed that all his little ideas fit together into one big idea. The professor taught Aristotle by building and building these ideas one on top of the other, building toward the Big Idea, which waited for us at the end of the semester. He even primed us in the penultimate class, saying the Big Reveal was coming tomorrow. I was excited. This was Aristotle, after all. I believed I would be learning the meaning of life. That would be tuition money well spent.

The day came and my professor tied it all together. I don't remember what he said—something about a Prime Mover. I was deeply disappointed. Listening to the professor describe Aristotle's vision of the universe was like having the rules to an elaborate game explained. The professor didn't even seem to care if Aristotle was right or wrong. The meaning of life wasn't the point. The meaning of Aristotle was the point.

I left the class with a calloused heart. Why had I taken this class? Why was I in this school? Why was I on this planet? I felt vaguely betrayed and thoroughly alone. Clearly, no one was going to help me. Clearly, not only *could* I do that, I was going to *have to* do that. Clearly, I was going to have to figure it out for myself.

I marched back to my room, to my stories, to my life, with no notion of the gift my professor had just given me.

TESTED

WHEN I WAS IN SCHOOL I had a very mixed relationship with tests. On the one hand, I disliked them, as did most of my classmates: I saw them as joyless measures of our inadequacy. On the other hand, I had every intention of doing well on every test, because to not do well would mean that I was a failure, and I could not bear the idea that there was any metric, no matter how meaningless to me, by which I could be measured a failure.

Numerically speaking, this position usually netted me an eighty-five out of one hundred, which, in retrospect, is an accurate representation of my commitment to the test. Occasionally, by the pure accident of personal interest, I would score a perfect one hundred. When these tests were returned to me I would feel first the rush of pride followed almost immediately by a total collapse of meaning. I had managed to answer someone else's questions accurately; the only pleasure this brought, thin as the paper my one hundred was written on, was the knowledge that at no point did this other person get to think: "Wrong. You are wrong. That is the wrong answer." *This* is what we were all angling for? This is why we were supposed to study and not watch *Charlie's Angels*?

My academic friends, who almost always scored one hundred on their tests, were quick to point out that doing well on tests was merely a part of the necessary game to get where you wanted to go. Unfortunately, though I loved games, I refused to play this one, and I remained a stubbornly B-plus student until the end.

I dropped out of school to end the tests, but I could not drop out of life. No matter how far I fell, I found someone who seemed to be holding a hoop for me to jump through. The promise always was that if I jumped through enough of these hoops, I would be allowed to leave the circus, a good lion returned to his rightful kingdom.

The circus can be a confusing place—all that cheering, all the lights and music. It is hard sometimes to know if you are in the ring or in the bleachers, if you are cheering or bowing, if you are dancing or playing drum. It is even hard sometimes to see that the one holding the hoop is you.

SIMPLY INTERESTING

THE WRITER MATHEW ALGEO does not believe writing non-fiction is particularly complicated. As he put it, the writer's main job is to simply find a good story. After that, he or she need only piece the story together in some intelligent way. What's more, he goes on to say, non-fiction writers don't even need to write the book to sell it; all they need is a good proposal.

I admired his point of view. It is easy to glorify what we do, particularly when what we are doing consumes so much of our time. If it is strenuous, if it is a mountain to be climbed, how much more virtuous that we are committing dark and lonely hour after dark and lonely hour to it. While tales of a writer's heroic journey can make for passable dinner conversation (maybe) and definitely good interview material, there is something to be said for keeping it simple in our own minds.

Tracy Kidder, who won the Pulitzer Prize in 1982 for *The Soul of the New Machine*, had trouble talking about his methods. "I don't know," he said. "It's what I do." This is a frustrating answer for an interviewer, but as a writer, I understood his point. For all the writing about writing I have done, the truth is my writing method is to meditate on what I most want to say and then find the most accurate way to say it. Pretty simple.

In my own work, what might appear complicated to a reader—if I, say, tie together two seemingly disparate ideas—is usually a product of patience. Often, the best stuff comes from doing nothing but waiting for my attention to sink below where I have been before, what I have heard before. When I am looking for that kernel of thought pulsing at the root of what interests me, I must do so with the faith that what I am seeking is simple, as simple as I—a single soul on the lookout for the next interesting thought.

WHERE YOU ARE

THOUGH IT CAN SEEM STRANGELY counterintuitive, the quickest way to change something is to first accept it. Or to put it another way, no matter where you may think you want to be, you are where you are.

For instance, there was a low time in my life when nothing interesting or satisfying seemed to be happening. This puzzled me. I felt capable; I felt curious; I felt creative; I felt ambitious—and yet, nothing seemed to happen. All was rejection and disappointment. During this period, I spent a lot of time living in my imagination. In my imagination, things were happening. In my imagination, I was having all kinds of marvelous success, meeting all kinds of interesting people, going to all kinds of interesting places.

I suppose I can't be blamed for retreating into my imagination. I was a writer, after all, and by necessity I spent a lot of time there. I learned to create interesting worlds in my imagination, so why not visit one such world if my world seemed less than interesting? It was a pleasant way to pass the time until things in my real world got interesting.

And then one day I was taking a walk, swimming as always in my imaginary waters, when something—literally—stopped me. Here I was making, and making, and making this happy imaginary world for myself that was really not making me any happier at all. It only made me happy as long as I hid there. I stood where I was, and I asked this question, "What could you make with *this* world?"

And as I asked this question, the world around me changed. I saw it all—the bushes, the pond, the birds—as clay. All of it was material. What could I make with where I *actually* was? Why not start there and see where it goes?

This is why every spiritual doctrine in history teaches acceptance. Acceptance is not passive. Acceptance is not capitulation. Acceptance is an understanding that to create, no matter what you want, you must begin by working with what you have, with where you are. If you resist where you are, you only create an imaginary world where you are not where you are. Everyone is an artist, and our materials are all about us. To use them, you must see them, and to see them, you must accept that they exist.

HOME IS EVERYWHERE

I GREW UP IN PROVIDENCE, Rhode Island, a smallish city in a famously tiny state. Rhode Island's smallness extended to its perception of travel distance, which said that Boston, a whopping forty minutes north on I-95, was too long a trip to make without very good reason. At nineteen, having taken a year's sabbatical from school, I found myself feeling penned in by Providence and its claustrophobic familiarity and convinced my closest friend to accompany me on a great adventure to London. He agreed, and six months later we touched down at Heathrow.

We found lodging at a B & B, which was really just a cheap hotel with communal bathrooms. And a bar. I was only nineteen, but this was Europe, where if you wanted to drink, then by God or whatever they believed in there, you could drink. One night I was sampling my first cocktail, a Malibu Rum and coke, when I heard a familiar sound. That sound was the word, "*Gawd*," spoken by a young woman—and then by another young woman. I looked up as a herd of them paraded by, all speaking in what sounded like but couldn't possibly be what is known in Rhode Island as a Cranston accent.

"Who are they?" I asked the bartender.

"Oh, they're from a school in America called Bryant College."

Bryant was located approximately twenty minutes from the Kenower family front door. They're following me, I thought. So my friend and I soon made our way to Dublin. We traveled by boat, crashing across the Irish Sea in the black of night and arriving in Ireland's capital at 7:00 a.m. on a Sunday morning. Dublin at 7:00 a.m. is a quiet place. So is its one bus terminal. My memory of that morning was that we were the only ones in that deserted depot. I was wrong. But sometimes you see what you need to see so you can finally have the experience you want.

Two years later I was back in Providence and bartending when in walked Tony Lee. Tony was a happy guy I had worked with for a few months when I was a senior in high school. We shook hands and said how great it was to see one another, and then Tony wagged a finger at me and said,

"Hey, Bill. Have you ever been to Dublin?"

"Yeah. I was there two years ago."

"And were you in the bus terminal on a Sunday morning?"

"Yes ..."

Tony smiled and slapped the bar top. "I knew that was you!"

SHARE ALIKE

ANY AVID READER, WHICH MOST WRITERS ARE, has had this experience: you finish a book and think, "I can't wait to tell my friend/wife/husband/mother/boss about it." In fact, the literary agent Donald Maass pointed out that this was how breakout bestsellers are made, by one friend dragging another friend across a bookstore and saying, "You've *got* to read this."

This is how we should sell books: as if we have just discovered it and can't wait to share it with the rest of the world. There is no purer motivation than love, no better stance from which to offer anything. "I love it; I thought you might too." It never feels like enough to love something by yourself. It is only the fear of rejection that restrains love's natural, gravitational movement toward others.

The ego preens in false modesty. Who am I to draw undue attention to myself? All stinginess and withholding is fear. As if our love of something could be contested by another's opinion. You will never know anything as clearly as you know what you love. It is your first and last knowledge, your guide, and your happiness. To withhold what you love from others is to judge them as unworthy of it. It is never for any of us to judge who is worthy of love and who is not. Give them the same chance you would ask.

And anyhow, what you love was never yours to begin with. What you love came to you, and you recognized it, and you asked it to wait a moment, and now you've helped it find a way to other people. That's all our writing is. We are just the conduits of love from that which gives to those who wish to receive.

BELIEVING IS SEEING

ON THE ONE HAND, I have always appreciated the maxim, "Seeing is believing." It is all very well and good to read about the Grand Canyon, to watch IMAX films of the Grand Canyon, but to actually understand the reality of the Grand Canyon, one must behold the thing itself. Reality is too vast to be communicated in something so narrow as words or images.

Then why are words and images so important to us? Why do we live in stories all the time—in movies, books, newspapers, online, with friends, at the dinner table? Because, in fact, seeing is not really believing. In fact, it is just the opposite. In other words, we do not believe what we see; we see what we believe.

My wife and I recently got into—I'll call it a discussion. It was a long discussion that neither of us wanted to have but both knew we must. As this discussion wore on, I began to view my wife as an adversary. She didn't care about me; she only cared about being right. As I came to believe this, it was as if she mutated. Like a wax figure, her face went from beautiful to ugly, and the edge in her voice became like the blade of a knife wielded against me.

Until I believed something different. Until I thought, "What if she actually loves you and doesn't want to blame everything on you? What if she's just upset because she doesn't understand what you're discussing any more than you do? What if that's why her voice has an edge? And what if you love her? Now what do you see?" What I saw was my wife, whom I still loved, who was as upset and confused as I.

If you believe the world is against you, you will see enemies in every shadow. If you believe people love you, you will see their interest beneath their every smile, within every polite greeting. Which is why stories matter so much to us. We tell stories not to describe reality to one another but to offer a lens, a belief, through which others may see a reality that pleases them most and serves them best.

PRACTICALLY DONE

LIFE CAN APPEAR TO BE DIVIDED in two: that which you must do, and that which you want to do. The musts are certain; the wants optional. There is bread to be buttered, roofs to be kept overhead. The march of survival tramps on unceasingly, and somehow, somewhere in the dirty, daily business of not dying we hope to squeeze in time for that which we most want to do.

Yet as someone who has spent many decades attempting to appease the beast of what must be done, I will tell you that his hunger is limitless. There is always something else you must conceivably do. And all for what? Some meager corner of your life you call your own?

Someone once said to me, "Bill, why don't you write a book like John Grisham, make lots of money, and then write the books you like to write. Wouldn't that be more practical?" In fact it would be impractical. I have tried and tried to do things I didn't really want to do, and I usually can for a time, until the tension between where I want to go and where I am telling myself I must go becomes so great that something snaps and I must start again with something else I don't want to do—saying to myself, "This time I will work harder, and be more diligent, and this time I will finish this thing."

Everything in your life is working tirelessly to get you to do the thing you most want to do as often as possible. You will be forever sabotaged and distracted and disrupted whenever you do what you don't want to do. No matter how simple it appears, no matter how logical, it won't work.

If you want to be practical, if you want to butter your bread, if you want to survive, then do what you most want to do the way you want to do it. It is the only way to ensure you will keep wanting to do whatever it is you are doing. You are the only one doing everything in your life, after all, and so if you don't want to do what you are doing, what you are doing won't get done, and I don't see what is so practical about that.

The Original Silence

I READ AN INTERVIEW with the actor Anthony Hopkins in which
he described teaching a class to UCLA acting students. Hopkins
advised the actors and actresses to do as little as possible. He
believed an actor needed to let the emotion happen as opposed to
forcing it to happen by tearing up all the furniture. Try to be still, he
said, and trust that the feelings are there.

How quickly advice within the arts dovetails together. I more
and more feel that writing is the art of what is not said. The most
delicious silence in the world is one filled with your audience's own
feelings. But how, one might ask, does a writer know when enough
is enough? It's fine not to overwrite, but who wants a dry, emotionally
inscrutable story filled with chopped phrases and bare stage directions?
Where is the line and how do you know when you've crossed it?

It is precisely because there is no line that writing is so valuable
to the writer. Were I or any other writer able to define the exact
perimeter of Enough, there would be no point to writing at all. That
you must discover on your own where that line is drawn is the

deeper reason you were led to write. Through writing you can learn the endlessly practical discipline of trust. You learn to trust because you are forever the judge and jury of all decisions in your life, and writing draws this fact into stark relief. You must trust yourself finally, or nothing will ever get written.

Strange with something so fundamental to our own well-being that trust has sometimes received such a harsh review. Do not mistake trust for naiveté. One assumes an outcome before it arrives; the other assumes safety regardless of outcomes. Within that stillness Hopkins describes lies an abiding trust that all you need is present in this very moment if you listen carefully for it. And when a writer pulls back her pen and says, "Enough," she has granted her reader a chance to listen also, having found a silence original to her, but available to all.

WAITING FOR AN ANSWER

IN MY EARLY TWENTIES, my brother John and I wrote and performed a show called *The American Basement Review*. The ABR, as it came to be known, was a collection of philosophical sketches loosely linked together in something we termed New Vaudeville. We always ended the show with a piece John had written called "The American Dream," which was a kind of dreamlike verbal landscape of Americana. I thought it made for a good ending because it was both poetic and strangely upbeat, just like our show. A little risky, perhaps, but we loved it all the same.

The more we performed the show, the better it got. I remember one performance in particular. Because we staged the ABR in small theaters, I could usually see the audience members in the front row. On this evening, there was an older gentleman sitting only a few feet from where I delivered the show's last line. I could see what remained of his gray hair, could see the wrinkles on his hands as he began to clap. And as John and I took our bows, I heard his voice, heard this man old enough to be my grandfather call out, "Yes! Yes! Yes!"

I don't think it would have meant so much to me if he had been my age, or even my parents' age. I had spent my young life looking upon men and women of his age as sometimes kindly, sometimes cranky members of an alien species. I could never quite glean where these people found meaning. Sometimes when I was feeling particularly judged, when I was feeling particularly lectured or scolded, I thought I saw in these septuagenarians' and octogenarians' eyes the smug certainty of someone waiting for me to be as disappointed with life as they were. It's called experience, boy.

Except you only ever see in others what you believe about yourself. Who was really waiting to be disappointed? My brother and I had found something we had loved and decided for the first time in our lives to share it with the world. Can you really do that? Is it really worth it? Are there really other like souls who love what we love?

That old man had my answer.

HONESTLY POLITE

WHEN I WAS A TEENAGER and a very young man, I was a bit of a Holden Caulfield type. I hated all fakery and dishonesty. I particularly disliked what I perceived as the ritualistic dance that was *polite behavior*. Not that I wanted to be impolite, but what if I didn't feel like saying "Hello" every time someone walked into a room? So what? Whose life was I leading? Why must I do anything so that someone else won't feel slighted? If someone was troubled by honesty, that was their problem, not mine.

But then I got a job as a waiter in a fine dining restaurant. Early on, I concluded that if I wanted to keep this job and make any money at it, I would have to master what I considered formal manners, the most restrictive of all behavioral expectations. I looked upon practitioners of formal manners as trained monkeys, actors in a play that they had, for reasons of upward mobility or familial requirements, chosen to perform until pulled from the stage by death or drunkenness. So what to do? Every customer is different. How can one know what is polite with each person? It can't be mere form. It must be something else.

I asked myself what every writer is advised to ask when starting a book. Writers should write the book they would want to read. I decided I would be the kind of waiter I would want to serve me. What I discovered was I wanted someone kind. I used to think that manners were a series of social maneuvers one memorizes so as not to embarrass or offend. But true politeness, I found, was just another word for kindness. All I had to do was to be kind. My kindness told me what to do. My kindness told me what to say. This was not so hard. I already wanted to live in a kind world where people loved one another. And when I acted from love, this is exactly the world I lived in. This wasn't fakery. This was honesty. My impoliteness had actually been *dis*honest. Love, I saw, was my only honest expression.

THE SEARCH FOR KNOWLEDGE

JOHN LENNON WROTE: *There's nothing you can know that can't be known.* I have to agree. I don't think anyone teaches anyone else anything. Everyone already knows everything. For whatever reason, upon entering the dream of life, we forget what we already know. And so, in this way, those people we call teachers are merely helping those they teach to remember what they have forgotten.

Sarah Orne Jewett said, "Write what you know." E. L. Doctorow countered, "But how do you know what you know?" Thus the writer goes in search of his or her book. And what do we find when we find this book? John Lennon knew the answer. We find what we love, which is all we can ever know.

Think of that moment when you find the sentence that brings a scene into clarity. Think of that moment when you read something that cuts right to your heart. These moments are part discovery and part recognition. In fact, this is precisely what I felt when I first saw my wife: discovery and recognition. When we see what we love, we discover what we have forgotten. When we see what we love, we feel both happiness and relief.

We are all teaching, and we are all searching. We search our stories for the core of love; as readers we search bookstores for stories that sound like love. We search the world for the people we love, the foods we love, the games we love, the clothes we love. We search and we search, and when we find, we remember again what it is to love; we remember again what it is to be us.

GONE BUT NOT FORGOTTEN

I WENT TO HOLLYWOOD based on the following logic: I don't care what I do as long as it's creative and involves stories in some way. This being the case, why not do something that makes me lots of money and places me right at the epicenter of American culture? That it took me nine months to see the folly in this thinking is the only surprising part of this story. Still, it was not a lost nine months. In fact, sometimes nothing is ever clearer than when seen up against its opposite.

My memory of Hollywood is of a hot, barren, strip mall landscape. I drove, and I drove, and I drove past brown hills and glittering studios and walls of apartment buildings looking for my big break. Everyone, it seemed to me, was using everyone else. As a part of an interview for a job as an assistant to a small studio, I was asked to watch three audition tapes and select the girl the executive "would most want to fuck." I didn't get the job.

In Hollywood, I was always trying. I was always trying to get a meeting, trying to get my script into someone's hand, trying to make money, trying to be in the right place at the right time. All this trying was supposed to land me someplace where I would be happy. That was the theory. In the meantime, more trying.

As it happens, I had carried a flame for a girl named Jen who lived in Seattle. Jen and I used to live in Providence, but she moved away when we were eighteen, and this broke my heart. Los Angeles is closer to Seattle than Providence, so I decided to call her. And then I called her again. And then again. I remember quite specifically hanging up after a long phone conversation with Jen and feeling the marked difference in my body, as if I had forgotten to breathe all those long hot days in Hollywood. I thought, "Oh, that's right. This is what it feels like to be Bill." When I talked to Jen, I wasn't trying to be a screenwriter, I wasn't trying to be rich, I wasn't trying to be successful. When I talked to Jen, I wasn't trying to be anything but happy.

THE PRESENT

I WAS GUEST LECTURING at a writing class when a student asked a question about one of my seven rules of writing: *Feel first. Write Second.* What, she wanted to know, should you do if you're trying to write a scene but can't seem to feel it?

The first answer, of course, is we don't actually want to write the scene, and our not feeling it is telling us so. More often, however, we *do* want to write a scene but are having trouble entering it. One of the best things to do in this instance is to find one detail that feels genuinely present in the scene—no matter how insignificant—and write it. The key is not to judge what you see. If you are trying to write a fight scene between your CIA agent and his nemesis but the only thing you notice is the pen in your agent's pocket, write the pen. Perhaps the pen will be used in the fight; perhaps it won't. Either way, it will serve as an opening, a crack through which you can enter the scene and then observe it, rather than try to make it all up from the outside in, to invent it with your thinking mind.

I thought of this shortly thereafter while having a meeting with my son's teacher. It was a long meeting, and there was a lot to talk about, not all of it the sort thing a father wants to hear. As the meeting progressed, my thinking mind, in its desperation to paint the world black or white and know with certainty whether this woman was capable of helping my son, began, as they say, to play tricks on me. One moment the teacher was a well-meaning professional with a heart of gold, the next a bumbling, taxed, depressed public servant just trying to get through a day without the children killing themselves.

Then I remembered what I had learned when writing, that I should never judge a scene through my thinking mind but behold it with my feeling mind, that it was my job to observe, not to decide. When I observed the teacher in this way, I was able understand, for reasons too many and too gray for my thinking mind to comprehend, that if she did her best, she would be fine.

It is the difference between a character and a caricature. The thinking mind *must* judge to draw its conclusions, but a true person is never all guilty or all innocent. You know this about yourself, and so you know it about others as well. The wholeness of life can never be known in thought. Yes, there are stories where certain characters, for narrative purposes, must wear their metaphorical white hat or black hat, but even here let the writer use these fictional poles to suggest what lies between. Whether we like it or not, we live within the wholeness of life—which is good news. A world without good or evil is the only place our heart will ever know peace.

SWEET SOUND

MANY WRITERS COMPARE WRITING to listening. I was reminded of this while watching Aretha Franklin sing "Amazing Grace" to Oprah Winfrey at the climax of her farewell bonanza. Think of the first lines of that song: *Amazing grace/how sweet the sound/that saved a wretch like me.*

The sound? Not the action, not even the word—but the *sound*. But it makes perfect sense to me. We are never guided by anything more directional than a sound. The pleasure of life, of writing, of all creation, is giving that sound form, turning that sound into stories, into businesses, into meals and kisses and conversations. If everything we wanted already had its form, where would the pleasure in life be? The next thing will always be more compelling than the last thing.

Sometimes I find myself in a room full of conversation, and I feel as if all I can hear is the sound of disappointment. The needle of conversation becomes stuck on what can't be made and the failure of what has been made. In my desperation to hear something different, I imagine I am a great singer and I pull a magic guitar out of my magic pocket and fill the room with a song too beautiful, too joyous, too poignant to resist. I sing the misery away and remind us all why we want to be alive.

Such is the dream of every artist, I suppose. Tune your instrument to me and we shall all be happy. Except it is no business of mine what anyone else is hearing. It is no business of mine how grumpy others might get on their way along the road. My only business is to hear what I am listening for and tune my instrument accordingly. I have never been unhappy while in tune, and it was only while deafened by the sound of my own complaint that I thought I needed to hear something other than what was already playing.

WHAT ISN'T THERE

DURING MY BRIEF TENURE at Concord Films, B Movie King Roger Corman's tiny but profitable film company, I had one opportunity to get close to the great one himself. His personal assistant needed two hours for a doctor's appointment, and I was recruited to man the desk. It was my Big Chance. Corman and I would fall to chatting, and being an insightful, streetwise Hollywood mogul, he would spot my intelligence and moxie—and the rest would be history.

It turns out my job was to sit at a desk ten feet from his closed door and answer the phone. The assistant whose job I was filling explained to me that unless the person on the other end of the line was one of Mr. Corman's children, I was to apologetically inform the caller that Mr. Corman was "in a meeting."

For two hours I answered call after call, apologized for Mr. Corman's indisposedness, and recorded the callers' names and numbers in a kind of ledger I suspected would never be read. I felt as if I had been recruited into the role of soulless gatekeeper in a Kafkaesque drama. The assistant returned from the doctor and reclaimed her chair. Corman's door remained closed.

Years later I was flipping through my son's copy of *Top 100 Horror Movies*, whose forward, lo and behold, had been written by Corman, who waxed nostalgic for the days when filmmakers were forced to frighten their audiences with what *wasn't* there. "It's [the audience's] imagination that does the heavy-lifting," he wrote, "not some digital effects house in Hollywood."

I have to agree with my old boss. We always frighten ourselves in this way—filling in the details of an unwritten future with nightmares we dream today. When the nightmares don't come true, we usually forget we ever dreamed them.

I can't think of Corman without seeing that closed door. Like so many executives, editors, and agents, he can easily become one of those monsters hiding in the shadows of his early films, a cold closed door of a soul, uninterested in the aspirations of new talent—not a busy man, hoping for a call from his children.

ALL WORK AND NO PLAY

MY YOUNGEST SON HAD GOTTEN TO THE AGE where if he were going to play, he would probably want to play with his friends or alone, but he had been having a lot of trouble at school, and it seemed to us he was not happy. How do you make someone happy who is unhappy? You can't. But you can help remind him what happiness feels like, and the best way we could think to do this with our son was to play with him.

Here is the thing about playing that I had forgotten: it can start anywhere. For instance, our playing began because one day my son was having a hellish afternoon. As a kind of joke and because we thought it might help, my wife and I forced him into a group hug. He decided it would be funnier if he didn't let go of the hug. So I said, "Let's see if we can walk together as a group into the bedroom without falling over or letting go."

We did. Then we tried traveling over the whole house. And then we tied our ankles together to see how far we could walk as a six-legged beast. And then we took the bandanna off our ankles, put it over our eyes and played hotter/colder. All because we made the joke of a group hug.

We are told that adult life divides itself into work and play, but I disagree. The point of play is to try something and see what of that something is of interest. The point of play is to follow your interest without judgment. Is this not what we do when we write? Yes, you want to be paid; yes, you are critiqued—but what are you doing but finding some kernel of interest and following it? Work is a mirage, an idea that life is somehow an obligation to be fulfilled. It is the word we invented when we decided happiness should be quarantined lest it distract us from the business of not dying.

Dig Deep

BENEATH MY SON'S BED is a four foot-long-plastic bin of lego pieces, a mass grave of disassembled robots, cars, trucks, and spaceships. From time to time I will spot my son squatting over the bin, digging through the legos like a dog searching for his bone.

I know what my son is doing: he's decided he wants to make something and he's searching through this multi-colored plastic soup for the exact right pieces. Yet if you knew nothing about legos you might draw a different conclusion. There are times my son's digging takes on a kind of desperation, and one might conclude that my son heard of a great treasure buried amongst these legos, a Golden lego, whose discovery will be the answer to all my son's worries.

The exact opposite is true, of course. Every single lego has precisely the same value. The wheels are only valuable if you are building a racecar; the windows are only valuable if you are building a house. If there is any desperation, it is from the fear that he will not find what he needs to create what he wishes to see.

The world is full of people scurrying about trying to make what they want to see. The pieces of our world are infinite: every blade of grass, every word, every mansion, every city. These pieces have no more inherent value than a lego cube. To dig for gold is to forget why you were digging, to forget that you were searching the world not for what you need but for what you love.

BLOW WIND!

THE RESTAURANT WHERE I USED TO WORK sat on the corner of Seventh and Union in downtown Seattle. This can be a fairly busy corner, particularly at rush hour, and at certain times of year a kind of wind tunnel forms through office towers and hotels, gusting west toward Puget Sound, inverting umbrellas and ruining hairdos. One afternoon, leaving the restaurant after a long lunch shift, I watched the following drama unfold:

A delivery truck was parked in front of the restaurant. The deliveryman stood outside the cab of his truck with a clipboard, adding the final details to an invoice. Beyond where his truck was parked, traffic flowed ceaselessly west along Union, the wind gusting and gusting, all of it, the wind and the cars, moving as one down the hill away from us to where I could see a small blue slice of the Sound.

His invoice complete, the deliveryman clicked his pen and tucked it in his shirt, lifted the brace on his clipboard—exactly as the wind gusted again, snatching the paper as if it had been attached to fishing wire. The invoice sailed like a kite over the truck and out above the cars, above a city bus. Miraculously, the invoice remained aloft, suspended on the wind over the river of traffic. The invoice did not drop down, it did not fly up—it merely traveled with the cars and trucks and buses, dancing above and with them as if it had finally found its purpose.

I watched as the deliveryman began his chase. I watched him running west down Union, trying to keep pace with the invoice, measuring a possible dash into traffic, even reaching out helplessly, as if he might summon it back with kindness. The invoice, meanwhile, continued its westward flight. Soon both deliveryman and invoice were lost to my view. I don't know how far and for how long the deliveryman kept up his chase. I don't know at what point he stopped running and forgave the paper for being so light and the wind for being so strong.

LOVE THY ENEMY

IN MY ESTIMATION, "Love the enemy" is the New Testament aphorism that will lose you the most friends. Yet it is one of my favorites. The entire quote could be paraphrased this way: it's all well and good to love your brother, but loving your enemy is where the spiritual rubber meets the road.

Which is to say, it's easy to have compassion for an oil-soaked pelican, not so easy a BP executive who would like this whole mess cleaned up so he, "could have his life back." But it is with the executive where you discover the true depth of compassion. Not that I want to be the guy about which it is said, "If you can have compassion for *him*, you can have compassion for *anyone*," but in this way, he is a gift to us all.

The same holds true for your writing. Gary Zukav described to me quite beautifully how growth occurs in that moment when you are feeling the "magnetic pull" of a fearful choice. Thus, writing is great when you're in the flow, the story is coming so quickly you feel as if you're taking dictation, but those days when *nothing* comes, or where everything you do bother to put down is only going to be thrown away the next day, that's where you not only learn about writing, but where you truly learn how to *live* as a writer.

When you spend a workday out of the flow of the story, you must choose kindness and compassion—that is the only way back into the flow of the story. You have written before; you will write again. But if you are cruel to yourself, if you tell yourself a better writer would have found the story that day, or that you will never finish the story, or that everything you *have* written is no good, then you will come to fear writing itself. You will feel relief when it goes well and despair when it doesn't. Love and compassion are your only tools when the day's work brings you nothing. Writers, in this way, must learn above all others to love *their* enemy, because a writer's only enemy is himself.

THOUGHTS OF LOVE

WRITERS OFTEN HAVE TO FORGET about history when writing about history. That is, the author knows what's coming, but the characters don't. In *Caleb's Crossing*, Geraldine Brooks's narrator cannot tell the story of a seventeenth-century Native American attending Harvard University with any knowledge of the violence and conflict to come.

Similarly, the tension driving Erik Larson's recounting of life in 1933 Berlin (*In the Garden of the Beasts*) derives entirely from the story's two central characters, the US ambassador and his daughter, not knowing that the men beside them in the opera and telling jokes at dinner parties, even the giant swastikas hanging outside public buildings, would soon be synonymous with evil.

Evil, however, is almost always a label for what has happened, not what is happening. We can't undo what we have done, and if what has been done hurts another, the temptation is to condemn the perpetrator to monstrousness, to strip him of free choice, to see his violence and crimes not as the expression of a choice, but of simply what he is, as if he had no power to choose otherwise, the same as a cat cannot choose to bark.

Yet in every single moment of my life I feel the burden and liberty of choice. There is nothing in the world that can be done to me that could deprive me of the power of choice. You could put me in a prison cell, chop off my arms and legs, gouge out my eyes, and still I could choose, if only what I am thinking. It is quite literally who I am. I am not my body. My body is a tool to express my choices, not that which makes those choices.

We call Nazis evil in part to make ourselves feel safer. Those men did those things because they *were* evil, as if they had been born deprived of the power to choose otherwise. They are different from us. They are monsters. And yet the moment I condemn another to monstrousness, even Adolf Hitler himself, I allow that it is somehow possible to lose the power of choice. If it is true of Adolf Hitler, then it could be true for me. The moment I believe in monsters is the moment I believe it is somehow possible to be prevented from thinking a thought of love.

UNANSWERABLE

IT WAS A SLOW TUESDAY NIGHT, and I was scheduled to get the first table. The restaurant, an upscale steakhouse, was empty, all 100-plus seats of it. Finally the doors opened and our first guest arrived: a tall older gentleman, the first of a party of two. Katherine, our host, asked if he would like to be seated while he waited. He would.

She led him down the stairs from the front desk and straight to table 33. This was always where we seated the first table. It was the most popular table in the restaurant—a booth, of course, centrally located. Better to seat it first, so the next and the next and the next won't ask for it. Yet it was also situated by the corner that led to both the bar and the restrooms, a fact I had never considered in my ten years at the restaurant—until that night.

Katherine dropped the menus and began scooping up the extra settings. The man, however, did not sit. He looked once around the empty restaurant, and then back at his table with an expression of disappointment and defeat.

"Do you have to seat me at the *worst* table in the restaurant?" he asked.

Katherine, a recently divorced suburban housewife who always spoke to each guest as if she were offering them cookies, began to stammer. "I-I'm sorry." She snatched the menus from the table.

"I mean *really*," moaned the man. "It's right by the *bath*rooms."

Katherine was already on her way to table 23. "How about this?"

"Well, *yes*," said the man. "Yes, that's better. I mean why would you sit me at *that* table?"

Katherine began to formulate her response, but the man was not done.

"Why me?" he implored. "Why me?"

Katherine was not at that moment equipped for such an existential request. She seated him, apologized, and wished him a nice dinner. Fortunately, in moving from 33 to 23 he had also moved from my station to my friend Blake's station. Blake emerged from the kitchen, surprised to see himself seated first. I was supposed to have been seated first. Seating order mattered to waiters.

"What happened?"

"Didn't like 33," I said.

"*Table* 33?"

I nodded.

"You want to take him?" Blake offered.

"No, thanks."

Blake eyed me suspiciously. "What's wrong with him?"

"We're all against him."

Blake sighed and rolled his eyes. "Why do I always get the crazies? Huh? Why is it always me? Why me?"

TRUE WEALTH

I WATCHED A VIDEO of a very famous writer who was spitting mad that someone would ask him to do something for free. His argument made perfect sense: the people asking him to do this thing for free were getting paid, why shouldn't he be paid? He detested the idea of giving *anything* away, and amateurs, he went on, who did do things for free were only ruining it for professionals like him.

Contrast this with James Bach, a lecturer and software tester whose business model is to do things for free all the time. Eventually, he explained to me, people offer to pay him for his services, and when they do, they pay him well. I like this approach more than the famous writer's, as Bach's key principle is the power of generosity. Both men, it seems to me, will make plenty of money, but only one of them is likely to enjoy it.

Desiring wealth is perfectly natural—healthy even. Everyone on earth deserves to be wealthy. However, I do not think you will ever experience wealth unless you live generously. That is, no matter how much money you have in the bank, if you do not perceive life's inherent abundance, you will only become more and more conscious of how you might lose whatever it is you have. No amount of money can insulate you against the belief that there isn't enough to go around.

Generosity does not mean donating to every charity that crosses your prow. What the act of donating to charities can do for some people is to remind the giver that there is enough in the world for everyone, and that more is always coming. *That* is the source of true wealth. And generosity extends far beyond the checkbook. Listening, for instance, is free and remains one of the most generous acts possible.

Somaly Mam, whose charity rescues girls who have been sold into Cambodian brothels, told me that while she constantly needs money, she would prefer never to be given anything out of guilt. Love, she said, is more valuable. When you give out of obligation, whether your time or money, the guilt you feel is not that you are lucky to have more than those to whom you are giving, but despair that you have succumbed to a meager of view of life, a place where the best you can hope for is to grab as much as you can, and then see what's left to toss down to the slow or unlucky.

A WILLING LISTENER

I HAVE ENDED MANY OF MY INTERVIEWS by asking the writer with whom I'm speaking what advice they would give to a less-experienced writer. While this is by far the most generic of all the questions I ask it is the one question that has remained essentially unchanged since *Author's* very first interview. I still find the answers as compelling as ever.

For although the writers appear to be entering teacher mode, appear to be speaking from a pinnacle—however high—of wisdom and experience, this moment is often the most intimate and personal of the entire interview. With few exceptions, the writers are talking to themselves. The advice they give are the lessons they needed to learn to find themselves in the chair across from me. The advice they give are often lessons they themselves must continue to learn. In that moment they become both parent and child, speaking backwards and with love to that part of themselves perhaps still not convinced that they have arrived at a destination that had once seemed unreachable.

I wish everyone in the world could be given a chance to be interviewed in this way. I wish this for the same reason that I know everyone has an interesting story to tell. Whether you grew up on the streets of Bombay or the suburbs of Philadelphia, you have an interesting story to tell. Not everyone, however, is ready to tell that story. Not everyone is convinced yet that their story is different enough, or exciting enough, or dramatic enough, or heartbreaking enough, or triumphant enough to bother sharing with another person.

Which is why my success as an interviewer will always depend on my willingness to listen without judgment. Everyone has their fears, even bestselling writers, and the open space offered by the attentive listener is the friendliest platform from which to speak. Sometimes it takes only one willing listener for a voice to feel heard. Sometimes, as on the page, the one listening and the one speaking are one and the same.

THE WASTELAND

ONCE, WHEN I WAS ABOUT EIGHT YEARS into a seventeen-year stint at a job I disliked, I turned to a coworker and asked, "Does any of this mean anything at all?"

"No," he said. "But the sparkling lights and pretty pictures keep you distracted."

Life had become a wasteland. I had followed a path that had led me to a place where nothing grew, where nothing I made came to anything. Even my wife and children, whom I adored, had become burdens of sorts, their basic needs binding me to a life I realized was the very nightmare about which I had long dreamed.

The mind plays tricks in the desert. Desperate for water and relief, it sees shaded pools where there are only rocks and more dust. Such a guide cannot be trusted to lead you out of the wasteland. The mind makes enemies of other artists, turning them into greedy farmers who possess all the fertile land. In the mind's desperation for answers, it narrows the world to a place of empty survival, where the fittest are allowed to stand a few more meaningless moments before being snuffed out just the same as the weak.

I would have been well advised to look more closely at those sparkling lights and pretty pictures. I would have been well advised to wonder where *they* had grown. The lights and pictures were not trying to distract me at all, but to awaken me from that nightmare. Within everything beautiful ever made lies a truth that belongs to the viewer alone. The artist's job is not to guess at that truth but to allow it through the inherent generosity of beauty, through that exquisite moment where he surrenders his ego in the service of what his soul requires.

Fortunately, the soul is as patient as eternity itself. The soul does not measure time in years spent in dull jobs or lousy relationships. The soul doesn't care where you've been or what you've done. The soul is a river forever flowing, and if you listen carefully, even in the driest and darkest of wastelands, you can always hear it. When you reach its banks, surrender to the current. You don't get to know where you're going, but you know you'll like it when you get there.

500 Love Letters

WHAT WOULD YOU DO if you had to prove that you loved someone? What would you do if in order to be with the man or the woman you loved you had to first prove to a skeptical third party that your love was genuine and not a convenient ruse?

This was precisely the situation in which chef/author Tiberio Simone found himself when he sought to marry his wife-to-be and gain citizenship in the United States. Tiberio had led a rough and dangerous life to this point. He had been homeless, a male prostitute, and falsely accused of murder. Not exactly an attractive candidate for citizenship, and precisely the sort of person who might fake a marriage to get out of trouble. So what do you do? How do you prove that you love someone?

Tiberio's proof was love letters. Though he had little formal education, during their courtship he had composed five hundred love letters to his fiancé, which he presented during his hearing. The immigration officials were convinced, and he was granted his citizenship.

Many years later, Tiberio would sit down to write his first book. He was much intimidated by the process. "I am smart," he told me.

"I know I am smart. Smart people like other smart people, and I like smart people." But was he *writer* smart? He did not have a high school degree, he reminded me, and he had never written.

"But you had," I said. "You wrote five hundred love letters." His face brightened with understanding. They may not have been ready for publication, but those letters directed him toward the source of all the best writing the world has ever read. All writing at its best is a love letter. Though often disguised as a poem or a story or even a blog, they are love letters all the same, proof enough of what we believe our lives are made.

BAD IDEA

SOMETIMES I THINK that the worst thing you can possibly have is an idea. Sometimes having an idea is like having the flu. The idea will drain you of energy and give you the sweats and send you to your pillow. Strange, isn't it, that this wonderful idea seemed to give you such a shot of energy when you first got it? You lie in your bed feeling betrayed, trying to remember the enthusiasm you once had for this idea's potential. Now the enthusiasm is gone, and all that remains is an impossible burden, trying to bring back to life something which appears never to have been alive at all.

When I was a freshman in college, an earnest and scholarly young man turned to me and said, "Bill, you seem intelligent. You seem like someone who likes ideas." I knew he meant it as a compliment, but at eighteen I already suspected that I did not want to be someone who liked ideas. I wanted to love life, not ideas, but the difference was beyond my powers of expression.

I had seen the difference. I had seen someone close to me tell me about his great ideas. The ideas always seemed perfectly plausible.

The ideas were always well thought out. The ideas could have worked. And the ideas never did. After the ideas didn't work, there was the search for answers. The answer, from my view, was always the same: the enthusiasm that had launched the idea dissolved long before the idea could bear fruit. Was this the fault of the person or the idea?

Neither, I would say. This same person had a habit of getting married and divorced and married and divorced. Each marriage was yet another idea for which his enthusiasm dissolved. Until one day the enthusiasm did not, and twenty plus years later he is still married.

There are as many ideas in the world as there are potential lovers. Ideas come to us as ceaselessly as strangers pass us on a busy street. To see the potential in an idea the same as we might see the potential in a stranger is perhaps generous but ultimately unworthy of our pursuit. Just because an idea could work, doesn't mean it will work for us. No idea can spark your enthusiasm. It is impossible. You *are* enthusiasm. An idea either matches your enthusiasm and allows its unique expression, or requires your enthusiasm to twist around *it*, bending your enthusiasm beyond recognition until all you've got is an idea—and no you.

WHAT ARE YOU DOING?

WHILE WORKING AS A WAITER I developed what is called carpal tunnel syndrome—or a very sore wrist. There was little I could do with my wrist that did not cause pain, particularly in a restaurant. Carrying trays of cocktails, delivering heavy dinner plates, even opening wine, brought a shot of pain from my wrist to my elbow. Even when I was not working the wrist bothered me. If I slept wrong it hurt; if I waved good-bye wrong it hurt.

I took measures. I wore a heavy black brace to work. I massaged it. I iced it. But it never got better. Day after day, month after month, and then year after year it only got worse. I never went to a doctor, never even considered going to a doctor. That was how I was. The pain was mine to bear. My attention was always on it in one way or another. The pain in my wrist was gradually becoming a part of who I was.

In the back of my mind was the notion that if I could just get out of that job, quit carrying those trays and delivering those heavy dinner plates I would heal. Or barring that, the pain would become so great I would simply have to quit. This life was grinding me down. My wrist had once been strong, but now it was weak. It had once been healthy, but now it was broken.

And then one day, in the quiet hours between lunch and dinner, I was chatting with the hostess. While we talked, I massaged my wrist. It's what I did. And as I stood there chatting and massaging, Michael, my General Manager, wandered by, looked at me and then at my wrist, and said, "Bill, what are you *doing*?"

I felt as if I had been caught talking to myself. All at once, I was sick of my wrist brace, of icing my wrist, of massaging my wrist. I was sick of living around this pain. I took my heavy black brace and threw it in my workbag. I decided the pain didn't matter. I decided I would work regardless of the pain, that I would make no allowances for the pain. If I was going to have to work every minute of every shift in pain, so be it. I couldn't control the pain, I couldn't seem to stop it, but I could choose not to care about it.

Two days later I was standing in the waiter station folding napkins. My wrist brace was at home. Folding napkins was another one of those repetitive chores that irritated my wrist. On this evening, I was midway through my stack of fifty napkins when I noticed something unusual: my wrist didn't hurt. I paused for a moment. When had it stopped hurting? I couldn't remember. The wrist had hurt me for two years, and yet I couldn't remember when the pain had ceased.

You would think I would be relieved, overjoyed even—but I wasn't. It was as if I had just noticed that a small scar had healed. I went back to folding my napkins, feeling as if, in some strange way, the wrist had never hurt at all, as if it had never been broken.

DOESN'T ADD UP

ONE STRANGELY COOL MORNING IN JULY, the local papers reported that we in Seattle had experienced only seventy-eight hours of summer—summer being defined as temperatures over 80°F. That sounded accurate. I had run my car's air conditioner twice and my bedroom fan three times.

Though I didn't know what this lack of summer meant to my boys. Whether it's 80 or 60°F, their schools remained just as closed. I understood the Mariners continued to play baseball beneath their retractable roof. My apple tree was bearing fruit, though grudgingly.

Summer is a hard thing to measure, I suppose. Many things are, though this hasn't stopped humans from measuring all we can, day and night. Growing up, my family would be watching football, and the fullback would dive into a pile, and from this scrum of bodies, after some wrestling, the referee would extract the ball. The chains would be called for, and the ref would have to lie on the ground to see that the nose of the ball was one inch short. Fourth down. And my sister would cry, "How do they know? How do they know it wasn't one inch closer?"

I heard a famous writer say once that if you write in a dictatorship, you'll know if you're any good because you will be jailed or killed. Such is our desire to put ourselves on some universal scale that he would invent this macabre metric. And if such a scale existed, if you could be weighed for literary or artistic value, would you put yourself on it?

You might be tempted. You might be tempted to finally know your value, for perhaps you've been uncertain. Perhaps there are days when you've looked at all you've done or will do and wondered, "What does it add up to?" Have you asked this question wanting an actual answer? Or have you asked it hoping secretly for the nothing that always comes in response? That nothing belongs to you, after all. It is your empty space where creation begins before it can be counted.

OLD WOUNDS

EVERYONE FEELS OR HAS FELT WOUNDED in some way. In fact, I knew a man who, when talking to me about his emotional writing fuel, complained that his childhood had been too loving and secure. That his parents didn't divorce or drink too much and that he had friends and generally enjoyed himself seemed to have wounded his chances for writing with real depth.

These wounds, it seems, are always at the hands of other people. The alcoholic mother, the cheating spouse, the abusive boyfriend, the violent neighborhood. Even my well-adjusted friend suffered the creative blight of parents who nurtured him selflessly. If only his father had walked out on his mother, maybe he'd have something to write about!

As writers we are drawn naturally to write toward these wounds. The heat of that which has not healed burns so strong it can drive a story on its fire alone. Oh, the power of injustice! We will march in the streets of our imagination so the world will know the truth. Yet even as we are driven to right the wrongs of our past on the page, we may find ourselves complaining of other people, the agents who won't respond, the moronic readership that does not recognize our talent, the narrow-minded contest judges. Our life would be just fine, if only other people would change their ways.

Now is when we must look again at those old wounds. What has ever been done to us that we could not undo? What was severed that we wish to rejoin? The creative spark that drives all writing, all painting, all music and industry and invention—if this spark could speak it would say, "You have never needed anything but me." If this spark could speak it would say, "There is nothing, no word or knife, that can come between you and me." If it could speak, it would say, "We are one and the same, and the wound you wish to heal is the belief that we are not."

THE EVIL MIRROR

ONE DAY WHEN I WAS TWENTY-SIX, I was visiting my wife's grandmother at her new apartment. The apartment was part of a complex whose units were arranged like a little village, set against winding paths, a playground, and well-kept lawns. The unit belonging to my wife's grandmother was on the ground floor, with a glass door that opened onto a little stone patio.

On this day, my father-in-law was also there to visit his mother. With him was his four-year-old son Ben, the product of a second, quickly defunct, marriage. Somehow the care of Ben had briefly fallen to me, and somehow, because I was not yet used to looking after four-year-olds, Ben had slipped out the sliding glass door and was gone.

I did not panic. He couldn't have gone far. In fact, I was so certain that he was merely out of eyesight that I did not bother alerting the other adults. I stepped out onto the patio and called his name. Nothing. Perhaps he had wandered up the grassy slope to the path. I climbed up to the trail and looked left and right. No Ben.

However, squatting on the sidewalk, outside the front steps of a nearby apartment, was a girl of no more than three drawing on the cement with chalk.

I approached the little girl and asked if a boy had passed this way. She looked up at me as if I were speaking French. I had just begun to understand the folly of asking a three-year-old for help when the girl's mother appeared on the front steps.

"Can I help you?" she asked in an odd tone of voice. People never used this tone with me. It was so foreign I didn't recognize it at first.

"I'm looking for Ben—my father-in-law's son. He's four. I think he might have come this way."

"No," she said quickly, shaking her head. "We haven't seen him."

I understood. I was the strange man talking to her daughter whom she had left alone for a minute. It can happen just like that. I began explaining that I was visiting Betty Paros, and I pointed to her apartment, but the more I explained that I was the hero of this story, the guiltier I sounded, and the mother kept shaking her head and saying she couldn't help me.

Ben had reappeared by the time I returned to the apartment. I wanted to drag him to that mother to prove I wasn't the kidnapper she had mistaken me for. I was haunted for days afterwards by the memory of the look in that mother's eye. Her eyes were a mirror of sorts, and in them I saw what evil looked like, and for that moment, it was me.

EVOLVED EXPRESSION

I LOVE THIS QUOTE BY WERNER VON BRAUN at the beginning of Thomas Pynchon's *Gravity's Rainbow*: "Nature does not know extinction. It knows only transformation." A great definition of evolution, I think, and I have always been a fan of evolution because it reveals life as constant motion toward. The question, it seems to me, is toward what?

The scientist might say survival. That is the equation of life. You live so you can live and then keep on living while you make more life that keeps on living. Everything from art to romance to French food is merely an expression of our biological need to not die. Yet I find not dying a hollow motivation to write. It turns all of creation into a contest to see who can forestall the inevitable the longest, a contest everyone loses eventually.

Rather a grim equation that, and so the Existentialist would say life is movement toward death. You know where you're going, friend — the same place we're all going, the same place everyone from Beethoven to Genghis Kahn has gone. Whistle through the graveyard all you want, that's the end result.

But what use is this to us? While I am alive I must get up every day and make choices. I cannot help this or stop it. I must choose what words to put on the page and what to eat and whom to talk to. Whether life is a movement toward death or not, my life in the living is constant choice.

My book moves forward, moves toward, with every word I choose. Every word I choose evolves my story. And as I look at that story, and the story that came before it, I can see each story living within the other. None of them dead or trying not to die, but each of them showing me the expanding potential of my choices, each of them transforming, word by word, the evolving expression of love.

SONG OF THE WORLD

IN THE NEIGHBORHOOD NEAR WHERE I GREW UP there were always boys who would drive slowly through the city in the summer with their windows open and their music playing loud enough that you could feel the bass line reverberating in your chest from where you stood on the street corner. You might have wondered what it felt like to be in that car instead of on the corner, but you would have been wise not to look their way in your wondering, for these boys would from time to time glare out of their open windows, and you didn't want to accidentally make eye contact and be mistaken for someone disapproving of their taste in music, no matter the truth of it.

It was tempting to judge these boys and this game of chicken they seemed to be playing with their music, but I had been asked often by my family to turn my own music down. The music I loved couldn't possibly be loud enough. When I found a song I loved, I wished I were an animated character whose body could dissolve into musical notes, that I wouldn't have to merely hear a song but could actually live it, could toss my own life aside for the one I perceived within the chords and chorus of the song.

This is what happens when you cannot yet hear your own song. You find someone else's and wish it were yours, and no matter how close it sounds to your own, no matter how loudly you play it, it cannot replace what you crave to hear. Moreover, what if no one else likes your song? Maybe you test the world with a song as you imagined you might sing. Maybe you play it loud enough for the whole neighborhood and glare out your window at all those people you believe wish to silence you.

I have never been so quiet as the moment I first heard myself clearly. Best not to speak then so as not to miss a word. Best to get still, for your wandering is over anyhow, the search ending in the same silence you once feared.

No Reason

I WAS NOT HAPPY, OR SO I BELIEVED. It was another day off to the job that was not writing, which meant I was a not a success, which meant I was not happy. Before I left for work that day, my wife begged me to listen to a teacher she had recently discovered. I did not like to listen to her teachers; I did not care what they had to say, I cared about getting published. But on this day, I said, "Yeah, fine. As long as it's short."

Right away, I liked this woman. She was funny, and she was talking about how human beings are creative and how this is what we do all the time, that this is what we were meant to do. Then she said something about happiness that I had never considered before. It was the exact opposite of what I had always believed, but she said it with such humor and matter-of-factness that I wondered if maybe it was true.

And as I drove to work, I thought about those times I felt happy. First I thought about winning races and winning awards. I thought about ovations and acceptance letters. The imagination is powerful.

Think something and it is as if you are living it. Driving to work, I could feel that warm hum in my chest I would feel at the sound of applause, or when I wrote a great scene. I had always called that feeling happiness.

But didn't I also feel it when I listened to "Hey Jude"? Couldn't I sing "Hey Jude" right now and feel it just the same? Wasn't it the same feeling as victory? And didn't I feel it when I laughed at *Seinfeld* or read Dylan Thomas? And didn't I also feel it the first time I met Jen? Wasn't that the same feeling as what I called victory? Wasn't that the same feeling I called success?

And then I arrived at work and parked my car and turned off the engine and sat there in the gathering darkness, thinking about happiness and music and Jen. It was time to go to work, but I wasn't ready to leave the car. I got very still and stopped thinking about anything, until I thought this: "And aren't you feeling it right now, Bill? Aren't you feeling it right now without any reason whatsoever?"

And work would never be the same after that.

DISCOVERING WINDOWS

I THOUGHT THE FILM *Julie and Julia* was unusual in its portrayal of the relationship between Julia Child (Meryl Streep) and her husband Paul Child (Stanly Tucci). Here was an adult marriage (they were long past the newlywed phase) that was believably and recognizably loving, equal, and sexual. It was my favorite part of the film, perhaps because I am in a marriage two weeks from celebrating its nineteenth anniversary that on its best days looks more or less like the Childs' marriage.

As I watched the film it occurred to me how rarely I get to see a marriage like this in movies. It is tempting to lament this. It is tempting to point out how ready we are to mourn the decline of the family and then race off to films in which that family is always laughably dysfunctional or downright destructive. But this would be unfair. Films, like all stories, are about conflict, and in *Julie and Julia* that conflict lay outside of Julia Child's marriage. In *Julie and Julia,* the marriage, it seemed to me, represented Child's indefatigable love of life and its physical pleasures, a love that would eventually see her through her challenges.

And because stories are about conflict, love stories will almost always be about couples, usually young couples, falling in love. Though I am no longer young, at least by Hollywood standards, I can find no fault in this either. Something in us grows up when we find love for the first time—that moment of recognition we call falling in love, that moment of seeing in another that which you have always felt in yourself. Such is the pleasure of creation: that which was inside of you is now outside of you and the world has changed.

If you marry someone, you only get to fall in love with her for the first time once. But I only ever get to do *everything* for the first time once. For instance, I only got to discover that I love to write once. And yet writing, like some marriages, can be a constant discovery. As with writing, love is not some destination but a portal, a window through which to see life as I intend to lead it.

LEFT UNLIVED

AS A JOURNALISM STUDENT, I learned to answer four important questions in my story's opening paragraph: Who, What, Where, and When. Thus:

Police reported that at 2:00 a.m. last night (When) residents in the Royal Heights neighborhood (Where) complained of shouts and gunfire coming from the home of James and Melissa Cameron (Who). Upon arriving on the scene, officer Peter Fauntleroy (more Who, sort of) found the body of Ms. Cameron sprawled on the living room floor with a bullet wound in her chest (What: Murder!). Officer Fauntleroy then discovered Mr. Cameron in the basement of the house, cleaning his revolver and running a load of very bloody laundry.

Then comes the fifth W: Why? Why did James shoot Melissa? There is also a sixth W—Will, as in: Will James be convicted? But isn't *Why* the most interesting question? Isn't that the novelist's question? All your characters are running around doing things— marrying each other, shooting each other, arguing with each other, buying each other presents—but why?

In this way, aren't we all mystery writers? Aren't we all puzzling out the why of our characters? After all, motivation always precedes action, if only by a split second. The action is like the crack at the end of an unfurling whip of motivation, and the louder that crack, the stronger the motivation. We may appear to be writing action, but we're actually only chasing motivation.

This knowledge has taught me well in my life away from the desk. When I find myself asking, "What should I do next? What should I do next?" I am often like a writer who is treating his character like a chess piece, moving this dead thing around the board of his story. There are thousands of moves I could make, and all of them seem right and all of them seem wrong. And so I ask myself, "What do I want? What do I want?"

And as I do with my own characters, I must ask this question with an open heart, prepared to hear whatever comes. It's so easy to think I know before I ask; so easy to think the mystery is already solved; so easy to leave unsaid what could be written, to leave undone what could be lived.

ALL THAT'S LEFT

I WAS AT A WRITER'S CONFERENCE ONCE when I overheard a woman mutter, "If I hear one more presenter say to write your book from your heart I'll just puke."

I could sympathize. This particular piece of advice has been so often repeated, its meaning has been worn as smooth as any cliché. Plus there is something naïve and toothless about it. Publishing is a *business*, after all, a business all we writers want to succeed at. Is this the advice you would give to an aspiring CEO or ambitious middle manager?

The trouble is there is no avoiding the fact that to participate in this business, writers must write books. And if writers must write books, from where besides the heart would these books come?

Could you write a book from your head? The brain is a deep warehouse of ideas and memories. The brain can memorize and follow rules and formulas. The brain can tell an apple from an orange. Unfortunately, the brain cannot tell us whether we should *eat* an apple or an orange. So many words and ideas are apples and oranges, and so much of writing is deciding between the two. To write a novel from your head is to be paralyzed with indecision.

So perhaps we should write from our loins. Is this not, quite literally, our creative center? Have not the loins spoken to us, loudly, of preference? What book would not benefit from that carnal drive, that itch, that delicious yielding to temptation? Sex sells, and this is a business, and we want to sell. All well and good, but for all the energy the loins provide, they can still betray us, not because the loins are wicked, but because they are disconnected from life before and after The Event. The regret of a loveless, post-coital bed bears the same emptiness as a book written only from this place.

And so we are left with the heart. The heart alone knows what you prefer, from lovers to fruit, and the heart alone seems to bear no grudge if you ignore it. Strange that such a mighty and all-knowing instrument should be so forgiving. The pain we inevitably suffer from ignoring our heart, from writing from our head or our loins, is not the floods and pestilence of an angry god, but the cramps and contortions of a soul twisting itself into something it isn't.

STARING

ALBERT EINSTEIN WAS SUPPOSED TO HAVE SAID that if he had an hour to solve a problem he would spend forty-five minutes understanding the nature of the problem and fifteen minutes trying to solve it. I thought of this when Andre Dubus mentioned one of his favorite Flannery O'Connor quotes: "There is a certain grain of stupidity the writer can hardly do without, and that is the quality of having to stare."

Which leads me to yet another great O'Connor quote: "I find that most people know what a story is until they sit down to write one." I believe this goes for writers themselves. It is not unusual to begin a story of any length feeling as though you have never done this before, that you don't actually know how to tell a story.

And so the staring begins. And what precisely is the writer staring at? Words? Not if he or she wants to finish that story. I realized recently that if I spend an hour writing, like Einstein and his problem solving, I spend only about fifteen minutes actually choosing which words will go on the page. The rest is spent staring at the thing I wish to say—or, more precisely, staring at what looks like, but is not, the thing I wish to say until it dissolves and reveals what I do wish to say.

In this way, staring is a great timesaver, because once I have seen clearly what it is I have been seeking, the words come very quickly. For this reason, when I think of writing, when I think of what it is I do at the desk, I never think of words. If it were only words, it would be so much simpler, for I would be like a carpenter building a story or an essay.

But I am such a craftsman only by necessity. Mostly, I am someone who stares. I am always staring at the same thing: that which I know but have hidden from myself. I have hidden it for a reason, and what both draws me to my desk and keeps me from it is what I will find, the truth I had forgotten for so long I had started calling it a lie.

REASSURING MYSTERY

YEARS AGO, MY WIFE AND I took our son to a neurologist to find out if he was autistic. Within five minutes of meeting our son, this very calm and experienced doctor looked up and said, "Well, I don't know why you're here. He's clearly not autistic."

Which you would think would be reassuring. Which, it was—but then again it wasn't, though it took me some time to understand why. Despite not fitting this doctor's definition of autistic, our son clearly had some challenges for which there was no predictable response. As we were leaving, we talked about the various strategies open to us—the books we could read and the therapists we could visit. When we reached the door to his office, the doctor paused, shook his head, and said of our son, "I have to confess. He's kind of a mystery to me."

That I found reassuring. I found my son's mysteriousness more reassuring than all the diagnoses and therapies and books and medications combined. How often have I been tempted to tack life to the wall and label it and know it as some museum exhibit or some Xray? How often have I wanted to put myself into a genre, or wear the hat of writer as if that's all I need to be? And how often has life itself resisted all labels but *living*?

Lisa Gardner said a writer's job is to become comfortable with being uncomfortable. I have never succeeded in understanding life through labels. All my efforts to do so have left me more insecure, more uncomfortable than when I started. That my son was mysterious meant I would have to understand him the way I have only ever been able to understand my own life: by trusting the direction of the mystery.

What other choice did I have? I have never known how a story will end, or who will buy it, or who will read it. I have only known that I wished to tell it. And even the story I am telling is mysterious, whose unveiling, like a life, deserves the full respect of remaining unknown to me until it is through.

CLEARLY BEAUTIFUL

I HAD A GOOD FRIEND who was a veterinarian and a father of four school-aged children. All his children were bright and got good grades and generally made their parents proud, but my friend was for some reason dissatisfied with their writing skills. The writing, he complained to me, wasn't beautiful enough. How could he get them to write beautifully, not merely functionally?

I tried gently pointing out that not one of his children had ever expressed an interest in writing beyond what was practically necessary to do well in school. But he wouldn't hear it. Beautiful writing, he was certain, could be taught. What, he wanted to know, was the writerly secret to beautiful writing?

Unfortunately, the secret is never what men like my friend want to hear. What we call beautiful writing only occurs when the writer cares about what he or she is writing. It is not really the product of training or practice or careful reading, although all of that helps in the long run, or helps certainly when the writers are not particularly compelled by what they are writing, as in, say, a school writing assignment.

But the beauty comes from specificity not stylishness, and the specificity comes from the writer's commitment to express precisely what they mean, not something else that is perhaps only a shade lighter but completely different nonetheless. There is far more beauty in clarity than raw originality, although sometimes in seeking clarity we are forced beyond the boundaries of the conventional to find exactly what we mean.

I realized this when I looked back at all the writing I used to call beautiful when I was a young man. It wasn't the writers' gymnast-like ability to pick an original word that drew my attention, but their underlying commitment to honesty and clarity that expressed itself in a way that was, to me at least, memorable.

So do not think about writing beautifully, think only about writing clearly and about what you care the most. Let the words take the shape of whatever your clarity demands, and then let it go. If you manage to say precisely what you mean, you will have provided another person the opportunity to share in what you love, and there is little in the world more beautiful than that.

The Safest Translation

THE MEMOIRIST HAS A TRICKY JOB: she must distill the entirety of a portion of her life—or maybe even her *whole* life—into one coherent narrative. She is in effect translating her own experience for her reader.

It occurs to me that translation is a good skill to learn, whether or not we ever write a memoir. Everyone I meet is something of a traveler from a foreign country to me, for whom I must find the best words and gestures so he or she might understand what it is I want to share. That we both know English is useful but by no means a guarantee I will be understood. No matter how intimate, we all remain strangers to some degree, isolated within the domain that is our unique perception.

It is a divide, however, that asks the best of us. While one can find commonality in outrage and despair, the truest bond, in fact the only bond that can sustain, is that of love. Eventually, one party will grow fatigued of outrage before the other, and the fraternity of fear will be lost. No one has ever grown tired of love. It is entirely impossible to do so; it would be like growing tired of breathing.

Love is the only bridge that truly connects us, inviting us as it does to set aside our fear of that which we do not know. Sometimes what we do not know is a new job, or a new city, or a new school, and sometimes it is a new story or a new neighbor, but the question to us in each instance remains the same: Do you trust this world or not? If the answer is yes, we find that the reach of love extends far beyond the husband and wife or the mother and child—it is the enduring promise of every moment that you are safe forever within the perception of love.

LIFE ITSELF

I CHANGED MY WRITING SCHEDULE ONE DAY. Instead of writing in the afternoon, I began writing in the morning. Not that I didn't get work done in the afternoon, but my children got home from school just as I'd be getting warmed up, so the interruptions began, and the flow would be interrupted.

The flow is very important. Writing is unlike any other work I have ever done in this way. I feel sometimes when I am writing as if I have plunged into a swift current. The ride can be exhilarating and interesting, but the engine moving everything forward is somehow separate from me. This is why writers often talk about characters hijacking their stories, or beginning a sentence and realizing by the end of that sentence that the story has changed completely.

I understand now that I both love and fear the current. The current is what draws me to writing and what, on my bad days, keeps me away from my desk. On the bad days I don't trust the current at all. What if it leads me to a quagmire? Shouldn't I know where I'm going before I jump in? On the good days, I'm happy to be along for the ride, and when it's time to get out, there's always a dock at the ready.

It's great to learn about dialogue and plot structure and crisp sentences—these tools help you stay afloat when the water gets rough. But writing is more about trusting the current than all the technical know-how put together. Eventually you must release your hold on the shore, and even the most skilled navigators can strike a rock now and again.

I have wanted to write to be famous; I have wanted to write so people would think I was smart; and I have wanted to write to make other people happy. It is obvious why none of these are reasons to write, but what was not obvious to me until recently was that I wasn't even writing to tell stories. Eventually, I, like everyone else, was going to have to learn how to let go of the shore once and for all. The closer I got to the water, the more I understood that nothing I wrote was make-believe, that the current I called a story was actually life itself.

ALONE WITH DR. KING

I HAVE BEEN TOLD that solitary confinement is the closest humans have devised to hell-on-earth. This does not surprise me. My wife recently read of a man who had been thus confined while a POW and that he and a neighboring prisoner had worked out a means of communication by tapping on the wall that separated their cells. This meager exchange became the prisoner's lifeline, what helped him endure the eight years alone in a tiny chamber.

Humans need to communicate with one another as badly as we need to dream. We are creatures that live by our imagination, and the world and all the other creatures in it feed that imagination and are in turn fed by ours.

The insomniac's bed is a kind of solitary confinement. If you choose not to wake your husband or wife or lover or call a friend, and if you are determined to stay in that bed until sleep comes, you are left only with the circling emptiness of the very thoughts that are keeping you from falling back asleep. I had just such a bout one night. It was a particularly vicious round, following a particularly vicious day. I was not going to wake my wife, nor did I feel like pacing my darkened living room. Yet every time I tried to turn my attention toward any thought other than those that haunted me, I found myself, as if lost in a hedge maze, back in the center of the nightmare again.

And so I asked for help. The first person I thought to ask for help from was Dr. Martin Luther King, Jr. King began telling me that I had nothing whatsoever to worry about. He asked me what I wanted, and I told him I wanted to help people. He said he felt certain I'd be able to do that but that being afraid was not going to help anyone and that there was nothing I needed to do other than what I already could do. He told me this over and over until I fell asleep.

I suppose I could have told myself these things, and I have in the past, but on this night I needed to hear it from someone else. I was tapping on the wall of my soul, and what I heard back reminded me that my loneliness was a misperception. Somewhere my imagination had come untethered and had begun to convince me I could neither hear nor be heard, and yet alone in my bed I was both.

WHAT THE THUNDER SAID

A RARE TREAT ONE MORNING as I sat down to write: from my desk I heard the sound like a truck rumbling in the sky, and I dashed outside in time for the next one to come. It was the sort of morning that would have been better spent listening to thunder than writing, but the sky went silent again, and I returned to work.

Growing up in Rhode Island, the summers would get so humid the air seemed to come to a complete and exhausted stop. Such was the price we'd pay for the guarantee of three to four cinematic thunderstorms every season. Finally the air would stir at midday, the clouds would lower to the treetops, and we'd stand on the front steps and wait for it. You prayed you'd get one right over your head, though the sound was like a crack opening to swallow the world. Still, there you'd be, intact, and then the rain would come and you could breathe again.

All that stillness before the rain could feel like death, even though it was summer and you had nothing to do, just as you'd dreamed all school year. A tireless nothing that strengthened with time and oppressed like the air, but to disturb it, to complain about it, would mean that you wanted more than this finally, your own time—not your teachers', not your parents', not your coaches', just yours—so now what to do?

What to do at your desk in temperate Seattle where thunder is like a tourist lost in your town? You feel like it's come to visit you from far away, because you knew it like the accent of a stranger asking directions. Here you aimed the arrow of your life at this time at your desk, and when the thunder rattles with memory and breaks the stillness, you run to it, hopeful for answers, and are greeted only by the silence you requested long ago.

ASHES TO ASHES

IT WAS SUCH AN UNUSUALLY COLD FEBRUARY NIGHT that I lit a fire. I love fires. I love building them, sitting by them, and tending them. I'm a very fussy fire-tender, poking, rearranging or adding logs every ten minutes or so. I pride myself on never needing more than one match to get a blaze going, and a fire that goes out prematurely feels like a failed experiment.

A good fire is the product of a healthy relationship between the wood. The logs must be close enough to share their heat and far enough apart to allow the oxygen needed to burn. The point is always the fire, of course, not the logs, and in a really good fire, where all the logs are burning, each log's flame lighting and re-lighting all the others, you cannot tell what log is responsible for which tongue of flame.

Still, I can become sentimental about the wood. Whenever I add a fresh log and watch its bare white wood catch quickly and eagerly, that new log becomes the king in my imagination. I look at all the other logs beneath it, coal-black and pulsing red, and remember when they were young and white and fresh and seemed eager to

burn. I watch as the old logs' heat lights the new log, whose fresh
flames in turn reignite the old logs, and I'm glad for the old logs that
they still have fuel to burn.

    I cannot become overly concerned about the individual logs,
however, or I will lose sight of their purpose. Everything in my hearth is
in service to the fire—the bricks of the fireplace, the iron grate, the poker
and the prong—all the hard things I can touch and move are there only
to allow for something that can be felt but not held, summoned but not
made, and which alone can transfix us as completely as a work of art.
The only memory fires leave behind is ash, which says no more
about the truth of a fire than a shipwreck does an ocean. In this way
the sadness of ashes is misleading, a trick of near-sightedness, as real
as believing graveyards are the sum of all creation.

MORE GREAT READS FROM BOOKTROPE

Invisible Ink by **Brian McDonald** (How-to / Authorship) A helpful, accessible guide to the essential elements of the best storytelling. Readers learn techniques for building a compelling story around a theme, making your writing engage audiences, creating appealing characters, and much more.

The Golden Theme by **Brian McDonald** (How-to / Authorship) A study of writing's essential commonality—the question of what makes writing and storytelling essential to us.

… and many more!

Sample our books at:
www.booktrope.com

Learn more about our new approach to publishing at:
www.booktropepublishing.com

Printed in Great Britain
by Amazon